Evangelization and Church Growth in the African Context

With Contributions by

Bishop Joaquina Nhanala
Rev. Keith Rae
Rev. Dr. John Wesley Kurewa
Rev. John S. M. Russell
Rev. Pierrette Ayité-Beugré
Rev. Musooko Moses
Rev. Sophirina Sign
Rev. Dr. Nkemba Ndjungu
Rev. Mande Muyombo

Africa Ministry Series

Evangelization and Church Growth in the African Context

Cover design: Karin Wizer
Cover photo: © Flynt | Dreamstime.com
Typesetting: PerfecType, Nashville, TN

ISBN 978-0-88177-745-1

Contents

Foreword

There are several books written on evangelization and church growth for the continent of Africa but this book excels them by its in-depth presentation of the subject. The writers come from different backgrounds and they present multifaceted content that takes into account several aspects of the African context, making it truly "Made in Africa" material.

In this time when the church is experiencing a tremendous growth in members and in the number of denominations, such questions like the "what," "why," and "how" of evangelism need to be addressed. This resource gives answers and guidance to these and other important questions.

We have before us the resource book written by African leaders, who are champions on matters of evangelization and church growth in Africa. The ideas and suggestions they present before us come from their personal experiences.

The writers are from Côte d'Ivoire, Democratic Republic of Congo, Uganda, Nigeria, Zimbabwe, and the United States. Their ministries have won them trust and respect in their countries and around the world. These include individuals such as Rev. Dr. John Wesley Z. Kurewa the founding vice chancellor and lecturer at Africa University who has written several books on the subject such as *Drumbeats of Salvation in Africa* and *Biblical Proclamation for Africa Today*. Dr. Kurewa gives his contribution to this manual with an essay titled "The Biblical, Theological, and Wesleyan Foundations for Evangelization and Church Growth in Africa."

The Rev. Dr. John Russell, who rose into various responsibilities in his annual conference, graces the manual with the paper with the title "The Future of Evangelization and Church Growth in Africa." The authors' experiences in pastoral work in local churches as well as academics are patent in their articles, which makes them very relevant.

The commitment of these leaders to "make disciples for Jesus Christ for the transformation of the world" has won the respect of many of us and their contributions to this resource book have given it an inestimable value.

I met some of the authors for the first time in Nairobi in 2000 at the first academy of evangelization organized by Global Ministries. During the presentations at this first academy, it became clear to most of the participants that more academies were needed to build capacity for more leaders on the continent. We also agreed that according to each conference's reality these academies should be replicated due to their importance for the reality of our church in Africa.

Global Ministries provided funding for subsequent academies in Mozambique, Nigeria, and Zimbabwe, among others, and a number of leaders have benefited from them and give testimony to their effectiveness as they apply what they learned.

The richness of the various presentations and discussions at the academies prompted the various participants to ask that a manual be produced to guide individuals and groups involved in this ministry. This resource book is a result of that request. During the 2012 meeting in Mutare, Zimbabwe, writers were selected to submit their papers for the manual and we commend them for their work.

The manual can be used in a variety of ways and settings such as seminars, academies, and other teaching settings. It can also be used as a personal tool for those with a heart for evangelism. I have personally applied the teachings/concepts I acquired from the several academies I attended when I was pastor at Matola Pastoral Charge and the results are that new preaching points were started and the numbers in some of the congregations grew and are still growing.

This is an "easy to read" resource book due to its language accessibility. It opens an opportunity for the average African leader to use it comfortably. It can be used as a tool for local church leaders and all other levels of African church leaders of any status or level of education. It is useful for both lay and clergy. This is the right manual for such a time as this in the African continent; therefore I strongly recommend it for all who have a passion for evangelism and church growth.

Joaquina Filipe Nhanala (Bishop)
United Methodist Church
Mozambique Episcopal Area

Introduction
Academies for Evangelization and Church Growth

History and Outcomes

When 11 persons from Africa, along with participants from other countries, gathered in Atlanta, Georgia, in June 1999 to take part in a global consultation on Offering Christ in the New Millennium sponsored by the General Board of Global Ministries of The United Methodist Church, little did we realize that we were laying the groundwork for the program now known know as the Academies for Evangelization and Church Growth.

The conversations held by the African delegates in Atlanta revolved around the need for more systematic training in ministries of evangelization and church growth. Even though the churches in Africa were growing at a tremendous rate, there was a felt need to be intentional in training persons.

The 1999 meeting had a very limited representation from Africa and was felt that this number should be increased to reflect a more representative group, including more women. This expanded group met in Nairobi, Kenya, in June 2000.

The purpose of the Nairobi meeting was to build on the formative ideas that came out Atlanta and expand on them. Staff persons from the General Boards of Global Ministries and Discipleship intentionally stepped back from being decision makers and focused on being listeners and facilitators at this meeting. Among the representatives at this meeting were the late Alfred Ndorcimpa, bishop of East Africa at the time; Joaquina Nhalana, bishop of Mozambique; and Daniel Wandabula, bishop of East Africa.

There was a great deal of enthusiasm and interest at this meeting. A broad agenda was set for a program called Academies for Evangelization and Church Growth. In the vision statement for the Academies, African delegates affirmed the following:

"Guided by the Holy Spirit, we commit ourselves to God to be the church that is prepared to offer Christ to Africa so that people may experience Christian maturity and fullness of life."

The Nairobi conference "resolved to establish Academies of Evangelization and Church Growth in each of the four regions in Africa in which The United Methodist Church is actively involved." The conference named several purposes for the training:

- Bring together Christian leaders involved in the ministries of evangelization and church growth from all the United Methodist churches in Africa.
- Train trainers who will, in turn, train others.
- Promote ministries of evangelization and church growth in the life of the church in Africa.
- Cultivate an understanding of the gospel that is to be shared and proclaimed.
- Examine the various concepts of evangelization and church growth as presented in biblical texts, in the history of Christian thought, by various theologians, pastors, and evangelists.
- "Fan into the flame the gift of God" (2 Timothy 1:6, NIV) that individuals already have for ministries of evangelization and church growth.
- Encourage participants to determine and select the ways of doing evangelization that suit their personality or lifestyle
- Contextualize the biblical and theological understanding of evangelization and church growth ministries for the African church.

- Impress upon participants the understanding that evangelization and church growth is the task of the whole congregation or that all believers are evangelists.
- Affirm the Wesleyan evangelistic heritage and its particular concern for the transformation of the whole person and the reformation of the whole society and its structures.
- Examine contemporary ministries of evangelization that are used by African congregations, denominations, ecumenical organizations, and other churches in Asia, Latin America, and the West.

Since the Nairobi meeting, academies have been held as follows:

- in West Africa: Sierra Leone; Nigeria; Côte d'Ivoire;
- in Central Africa: Democratic Republic of Congo (Kinshasa and Lubumbashi);
- in Eastern Africa: Kenya; and
- in Southern Africa: Mozambique and Zimbabwe.

Curriculum of the Academies

The overall vision of the academies is to use a train-the-trainer methodology that focuses on the African context.

The academies have included such themes as:

- conflict resolution;
- poverty;
- health;
- African religions and Islam;
- economic, social, and political issues;
- women, children, and youth;
- justice, war, and peace;

- culture;
- Wesleyan theology and evangelization and church growth;
- leadership; and
- stewardship.

Outcomes of the Academies

Over the years it is safe to estimate that more than 500 people were directly trained using the train-the-trainer methodology.

The following are some outcomes of the academies:

- In Sierra Leone, a three-year program for training evangelists was put in motion.
- In Liberia, resources were produced and used in follow-up workshops.
- In the Democratic Republic of Congo, two persons who participated in the academies went on to study at Africa University and received their degrees in theology.
- In Zimbabwe and other places new churches were established and existing congregations were strengthened.
- In Nigeria, the curriculum was used in the syllabus of one of the Bible schools.

Churches participating in the academies share common concerns, which transcended language, culture and religion. These included gospel and culture framed in questions like those listed below:

- How can I be Christian and African?
- What are the positive aspects of African culture that can be incorporated in the proclamation of the gospel?
- How do Africans incorporate aspects of traditional religion into Christian faith and practice?

Through the academies, a core of leaders emerged and brought their expertise in theology, biblical studies, culture, and political, social, and economic studies to churches in Africa. Themes were discussed at the academies that did not have a place on the meeting agendas at conference or district levels.

Another significant outcome of the academies was providing a model for similar academies, which were held in Thailand and Eurasia. What began as an African program has since moved to other countries.

An additional outcome of the academies is that African leadership took full responsibility for developing and implementing them and as a result there was African ownership of the academies. African leaders brought their cultural, social, political, and economic ideas to the academies.

This demonstrated that there are human resources in African churches, which could with financial coordination and other assistance, conduct this program.

The Role of Global Ministries

It should be clear that the academies are not a program of Global Ministries. It is a genuinely African program, conceptualized and implemented by African church leaders.

This does not mean that Global Ministries does not play an important role. Global Ministries assists by providing financial backing as well as coordination. It also brings leaders together via teleconferences to make plans and to lay the groundwork for the academies.

Do You Want to Plan an Academy in Your Conference?

Bishops played a key role by naming persons who formed the core leadership for the planning of an academy. The bishop(s) would appoint three or four persons to work with Global Ministries' staff to do the following:

- Identify an overall theme and three or four sub-themes, which would form the curriculum of the academy. These themes would relate to the context of their country or countries.
- Select persons to present the themes.
- Select persons to attend the academy.
- Develop a budget.
- Plan the program.
- Select Bible study leaders.
- Develop an evaluation of the academy.
- Select worship leaders.
- Make travel plans.
- Select leadership to chair daily meetings as well as lead in worship.

This model can also be used for mini-academies or follow-up academies. It also can be used in any context or country with appropriate variations and sensitivity to cultural norms and values.

Why a Resource Book?

Faced with diminishing financial resources from Global Ministries, a group representing United Methodist churches in Africa met at Africa University in June 2012. They recommended that a resource be produced that would accomplish the following:

- provide a permanent record of some of the themes, which have been addressed in previous academies;
- serve as a primary document for presenters who could use it along with other supplementary materials;
- minimize the need for additional funding to continue the academies;
- be available in the majority language of the country;
- serve as an inexpensive resource if it was made available on the web;

- be available for clergy and lay persons, lay academies, pastors' schools, seminaries, and Bible colleges; and
- be a resource to equip, empower, and enable The United Methodist Church in Africa.

Contents of the Resource Book

The Africa University meeting reviewed the themes presented at previous academies and selected those which were echoed throughout the continent.

The meeting also recommended that writers should reflect the continental nature of The United Methodist Church in Africa and that special attention should be given to selecting women to write some of the articles.

How to Use the Resource Book

We hope that this text will be a valuable resource for continuing to train persons in ministries of evangelization and church growth. You can use this resource tool to provoke your interest on the topic.

- Look at the article from your own context and see what meaning it has for you.
- Raise questions that emerge from the article.
- Discuss it with your friends and colleagues.
- Build on this resource book by adding other themes, which are critical in your context.

You can use any essay in this resource for your academy.

The resource book does not cover all of themes presented at the academies. There are important omissions such as poverty and health.

It will be translated into French and Portuguese.

Keith Rae is a retired member of the New England Conference where he served churches in Massachusetts, Connecticut, and Rhode Island. He served as a Global Ministries staff person from 1982-2006 and as a Global Ministries consultant from 2009-2014. He and his wife Veronica have three children and six grandchildren.

1

The Biblical, Theological, and Wesleyan Foundations for Evangelization and Church Growth in Africa

Introduction

For the past half-century, various church leaders and scholars of Africa have made predictions about church growth in Africa. In his opening speech at the Eighth Assembly in Harare, then general secretary of the World Council of Churches, Konrad Raiser said, "By the early part of the 21st century, Africa promises to be the continent with the largest Christian population."[1]

The Population Reference Bureau notes the explosive growth of the continent:

Africa, by far the world's poorest region, will record the largest amount of population growth of any world region between now and 2050.

Africa's population is expected to more than double, rising from 1.1 billion today to at least 2.4 billion by 2050.[2]

As a starting point, I will begin by defining the terms evangelization and church growth.

First, in defining the term evangelization, it is often helpful to note a distinction between, as well as its relationship with the term evangelism, in this presentation. Evangelism is a specific ministry of the church that primarily focuses on sharing or communicating the gospel of Jesus Christ to others. In the Wesleyan tradition, such communication of the gospel to people, which may lead to conversion, leads the convert toward

Christian perfection or Christian maturity. The term evangelization is broader in scope or more comprehensive than the term evangelism. In evangelization, other ministries of the church come into play: ministries such as worship, Christian education, Christian social concerns, and many others. Therefore, the term evangelization embraces all the ministries or activities of the church that enable a Christian to grow in the Christian faith.

From the beginning, missionary evangelization of Africa included evangelism, education, health care, agriculture (the gospel of the plow as some early African Christians in Zimbabwe called it), carpentry, building or masonry. From the 1960s through the 1980s, theologians of the Third World seemed to have come to a consensus that the term evangelization had to be understood as an umbrella concept embracing the whole activity of the church sent into the world:

> "One single term—evangelization—defines the whole of Christ's office and mandate" (EN 6;cf Snijders 1977:1972; Geffre 1982:489; Scherer 1987:205). In like manner, Geijbels (1978:73-82) understands evangelization to include proclamation, translation, dialogue, service, and presence. And Walsh (1982:92) states that "human development, liberation, justice, and peace are *integral* parts of the ministry of evangelization."[3]

The Third Assembly of the All African Conference of Churches, held in Lusaka, Zambia, in 1974 resolved that:

> The Church should regard evangelization as the total witness, in word and deed to the whole life of persons and communities leading to liberation and fullness of life.[4]

In defining the term church growth, there is need to understand church growth as a natural phenomenon just as a child who is born today is expected to grow. While in some societies there may be a baby boom or a baby scarcity; there can be also church growth or stagnation. It is important that the churches in Africa understand where and how the Church is growing on the continent. Paul Gifford reports on a survey that was conducted by the Ghana Evangelism Committee of the entire country in 1986-1987, and repeated in 1993. A comparison of the two surveys was most revealing.

> The AIC [African Independent Churches] are in serious difficulty [on the decline]; the mainline churches are static if not decreasing [a good number were on the decline, just a few that were on the increase]; and substantial growth lies with new Pentecostal and "mission-related churches" [a massive percentage of growth of Christians lies here].[5]

The changes monitored over a five-year period in Ghana, would support the impression given in many countries in Africa. At the same time, while the mainline churches position was reported as static in terms of the percentage average, the churches such as the Presbyterian Church had an increase of 17 percent; and the Methodist Church of Ghana also had an increase of 2 percent. Because the other mainline churches registered a decrease, the overall mainline average percentage was 7 percent; while the highest of the Pentecostal churches[6]—the Assemblies of God—had an increase of 87 percent. Also note that, while the Assemblies of God grew to 60,298 members, the Methodist Church of Ghana grew to 188,727. This is the kind of research or survey that all church councils in Africa should be encouraged to conduct.[7]

We should be driven to understand the term church growth as not only numerical growth, but also as a natural result of the evangelization programs that are taking place in Africa.

Biblical Foundation for Evangelization and Church Growth

God calls a people or individuals for a purpose and always for his mission. Thus the Judeo-Christian understanding of any chosen people is not necessarily for their benefit alone; rather it is always for the purpose of carrying out God's plan of evangelization. Although there are several examples of people called for God's mission in the Bible, I shall select four examples, two from the Old Testament and two from the New Testament.

First, the call of Abraham:

> Leave your country, your people and your father's household and go to the land I will show you. I will make you into a great nation and I will bless you; I will make your name great, and you will be a blessing. I will bless those who bless you, and whoever curses you I will curse; and all peoples on earth will be blessed through you. (Genesis 12:1-3 NIV)[8]

God spoke to Abraham when he was still in his country, Mesopotamia. Terah, Abraham's father, and his tribesmen were nomadic people.[9]

Religiously, we understand it was "the god Nannar or Sin, the moon-god who was so prominently worshipped;"[10] and it was in that kind of cultural context that the Lord called Abraham, to come out, when he was then, known as Abram. The call of Abraham was a call to create a people for a divine purpose.[11] God promised Abraham a sevenfold structure: to make him into a great nation, to bless him, to make his name great, to make him a blessing, to bless those who bless him, to curse whoever curses him, and to bless all peoples on earth through Abraham. In short, the call of Abraham by God was to be a blessing to all the people on earth.

The second Old Testament example is Isaiah, who first shared the theological insight that Israel had been called by God to be light to the world.

> It is too small a thing for you to be my servant to restore the tribes of Jacob and bring back those of Israel I have kept. I will also make you a light for the Gentiles, that you may bring my salvation to the ends of the earth. (Isaiah 49:6)

"Together with Gen. 12:1-3; Ex. 19:5-6, this verse [Isaiah 49:6] is sometimes called the 'great commission' of the OT."[12] Paul and Barnabas quoted Isaiah when they addressed the Jews at the synagogue of Pisidian Antioch, as they left the Jews alone and went to proclaim Christ to the Gentiles (Acts 13:47). This text of Second Isaiah is so important because the emphasis of its message is that:

Israel's mission extends beyond the confines of her own people [49:1-5] to the nations of the world . . . [and that was] an end, once and for all, to the idea that Israel's sole duty is its own salvation.[13]

The fact that Jesus said he had not come to abolish the Law and the Prophets, but to fulfill them (Matthew 5:17). This shows that there was still something in Israel that needed regeneration. It took God to perform that regeneration, and indeed, Jesus came to do what no mortal man could have done. There was a sense in which Judaism proved to be "a light for the Gentiles." Several non-Jewish people were attracted to the ethical monotheism of Judaism, and its observation of the Sabbath and the strong sense of family life.[14] That attraction led to proselytism—the process of converting persons from one religion to another religion. Hence Jesus' reference to the teachers of the law and Pharisees who traveled over land and sea to win a single convert (Matthew 23:15).

Third, in the New Testament Jesus of Nazareth, who emphasized he had ben sent by his father (John 3:34; 20:21), inaugurated the kingdom of God on earth through evangelization. "Jesus went throughout Galilee, teaching in their synagogues, preaching the good news of the kingdom, and healing every disease and sickness among the people" (Matthew 4:23).

Jesus embraced all persons as he proclaimed the message of the kingdom of God, including those who would be excluded according to the law (Leviticus 21:18-19):

> The Spirit of the Lord is on me, because he has anointed me to preach good news to the poor. He has a sent me to proclaim freedom for the prisoners and recovery of sight for the blind, to release the oppressed, to proclaim the year of the Lord's favor. (Luke 4:18-19)

From among his disciples, Jesus chose the Twelve, whom he also designated or ordained apostles (Luke 6:13). The Twelve, minus Judas Iscariot, became pillars to Jesus' witness throughout the world. They had been with Jesus beginning with John's baptism to the time when Jesus was taken away from them (Acts 1:21-22). These were the men who received the commission from the risen Christ to ". . . go and make disciples of all nations" (Matthew 28:19); "go into all the world and preach the good news to all creation" (Mark 16:15); "and repentance and forgiveness of sins will be preached in his name to all nations, beginning at Jerusalem" (Luke 24:47); and, ". . . as the Father has sent me, I am sending you" (John 20:21).

Fourth, after receiving the promised gift of the baptism of the Holy Spirit on the day of Pentecost, God added to their number Paul of Tarsus, who did not see Jesus in flesh, but saw him, "as one abnormally born" (1 Corinthians 15:8). Paul vividly, testified:

But when God, who set me apart from birth and called me by his grace, was pleased to reveal his Son in me so that I might preach him among the Gentiles, I did not consult any man, nor did I go up to Jerusalem to see those who were apostles before I was, but went immediately into Arabia and later returned to Damascus. (Galatians 1:15-17)

Those were the leaders of the early church, and included among them were women, who proved themselves to be staunch witnesses to Jesus Christ:

- the women who were "near the cross" at Jesus' crucifixion—Mary his mother, his mother's sister, Mary the wife of Clopas, and Mary Magdalene (John 19:25);
- Mary Magdalene, according to John, who first witnessed to the 11, "I have seen the Lord!" (John 20:18);
- Mary, the mother of John Mark, who turned her house into a house of prayer as Herod breathed fire on the Twelve;
- Rhoda, a servant girl, who went to answer the door when Peter knocked, but forgot to open it due to excitement (Acts 12:13);
- Lydia in Philippi, who shared her hospitality to Paul and Silas amidst hostilities (Acts 16:15); and
- Priscilla and her husband Aquila in Ephesus, who knew how to expound the gospel to others adequately (Acts 18: 26).

Theological Foundation for Evangelization and Church Growth

The transmission of faith from one generation to another has always recognized the role of sound theology, which ultimately enables the production of sound doctrine. In African religions, practically all that has been transmitted from generation to generation has been conveyed through oral tradition that embraces storytelling, rituals, riddles, proverbs, and many other methods. Admittedly, there are some similarities with how both the Old and New Testament witness was communicated before the formation of the Bible. While the prophets of the Old Testament wrestled with trying to understand the will of God, the apostles and their followers witnessed about what they saw and heard from Jesus himself. Hence John wrote:

That which was from the beginning, which we have heard, which we have seen with our eyes, which we have looked at and our hands have touched—this we proclaim concerning the Word of life. (1 John 1:1)

As that Christian faith was communicated through preaching, it demanded that it also be taught to new converts. Thus the teaching ministry or what is today called Christian education became a vital aspect of evangelization with each generation of Christians. It became the task of sound theology to deliver sound doctrine.

In the 18th century, missionary churches that came to Africa from the Western nations followed the same pattern of establishing institutions. We came to understand these as mission stations or mission compounds, from which the task of the evangelization of Africa was launched. Different church denominations used various methods of evangelization, including evangelism, education, medical care, and various types of technical education.[15] Currently, evangelization in theological education (Christian education) for the church members and theological education and training for the ordained ministry has received great attention.

African Religion and Church Growth

African belief in God, imperfect as it was prior to the coming of Christianity is proving to be a sound theological explanation for church growth in Africa today. African knowledge about God now stands tall claiming to be the stone that the Western builders of the church in Africa rejected, but has now become the cornerstone (Acts 4:11). Today, as African Christianity reflects and expresses itself through an African lens, their reaction to the good news of Christ, the Son of God, sounds like, "Welcome home; for we have been waiting a long time for you!" Indeed the African people have always known something about God. If they were in darkness, even to the extent of becoming darkness themselves (Ephesians 4:18), it was because, like the rest of humanity, they did not know God, the Creator through Jesus Christ.

Wherever the Christian faith is received, properly understood, and allowed to wear the African religious jacket (in worship, prayer, preaching, fellowship, and other aspects), it is thriving. Sadly, though, wherever Christianity continues to wear the Western jacket in the African church, it may mean that such African Christians are being deprived of the opportunity to be genuine African children of God, who can cry in their mother language, "A*bba*, Father." And such churches may be dwindling in numbers.

Incarnational Evangelism and Church Growth

A student for the Master of Arts Degree in Evangelism at Africa University, Alfred Karimu from Sierra Leone, who is studying Islam in West Africa as a special subject, shared in one of our class discussions:

Muslims have no missionaries who go back home; when they come to a country or community, they come to stay. That way the Muslims share not only their message about Islam . . . they also share their lifestyle in their new community. As vigorous traders as they are, Muslims open shops, factories and other business enterprises for their support—and offer opportunities of employment to people of their new community.[16]

Naturally, this led me to think of incarnational evangelism:

> The Word became flesh, and made his dwelling among us. We have seen his glory, the glory of the One and Only, who came from the Father, full of grace and truth. (John 1:14)

The words of my student took me back to an experience I had in my first appointment as a pastor at Chikwizo Circuit with *Baba* (Dad) Kateera. Baba Kateera was a man of great faith in God. Chikwizo Circuit is in the Mutoko District in northeastern Zimbabwe. Baba Kateera was from Mutoko, the capital of the Mutoko District. Although The United Methodist Church has the Mutoko Mission there, Baba Kateera and his wife left Mutoko for Chikwizo, where he was appointed as a teacher. When he retired in 1953, the couple decided to settle in Chief Chikwizo's area.[17] Having been given a piece of land on which to settle and cultivate, he did wonders. Chikwizo is in an area of Zimbabwe that is dry, and receives very little rain. As a man who loved agriculture, he grew crops that were drought resistant, such as different types of millet, ground nuts, and watermelons, and he planted many fruit trees such paw-paw trees, and others. In spite of the scarcity of rain in the area, Baba Kateera had a good harvest almost every year. He helped those who sought his assistance and he gave away food to many needy families, including the teachers who were in that area.

Baba Kateera believed he was a missionary; that he was to be the light to the people in Chikwizo and to help the local people. He was indeed a missionary, but he was a missionary who was not on salary and had no plans to return to Mutoko where he was born and raised. Above all, he was a missionary who shared the good news of Christ, not only through his words, but also through his lifestyle that led away from a dependency that many missionary churches suffer today. Baba Kateera shared the Christ like life: "I have come so that they may have life, and have it to the full" (John 10:10).

Wesleyan Foundation for Evangelization and Church Growth

The preaching and teaching of John and Charles Wesley was solidly grounded upon centuries of Christian heritage doctrine. The fundamental doctrines of Christianity: creation, the Trinity, the incarnation, atonement, the Church and all others were presupposed in all the evangelistic preaching, teaching, and singing of the people called Methodists. Among those Christian doctrines, John Wesley placed special emphasis on particular doctrines:[18]

Our main doctrines, which include all the rest are three—that of repentance, of faith and of holiness. The first of these we account as it were, the porch of religion; the next, the door; the third, religion itself.[19]

John Wesley perceived a dynamic movement of the gospel in these doctrines that he identified as "the scriptural way to salvation" or "the order of salvation." Philip Watson aptly stated the message embraced in these doctrines: "(1) All men need to be saved; (2) all men can be saved; (3) all men can know that they are saved; (4) all men can be saved to the uttermost."[20]

When the Wesleyan Revival was launched in England in the 18th century, some of the early Methodists there were nurtured in the Puritan tradition that taught predestination from a strict Calvinist perspective.[21]

In contrast, both John and Charles "rejected predestination root and branch . . . The restriction of God's grace to the elect few was utterly repugnant to their understanding of the New Testament, and made nonsense of the moral spiritual life."[22] Hence the Methodists sang one of Charles' hymns: "For all, for all, my Savior died."[23] The heart of the message in the Wesleyan Revival was, "God wills all men to be saved, and that Christ died for all, so that all may come to him and be saved, if only they will."[24]

The message of the Wesleyan Revival was characterized with the profundity of God's grace, and the goal was not so much as achieving numerical growth of converts or expansion as much as that was important too; rather the primary goal and thrust of the Wesleyan Revival was to see people converted to Christ, and to enable them grow to Christian perfection.[25] "Be perfect, therefore, as your heavenly Father is perfect" (Matthew 5:48). Today we understand this kind of growth as the spiritual growth of

Christians. The Wesleyan Revival sought to achieve that goal of Christian perfection by ministering to its converts through a three-fold ministry, namely: preaching and teaching emphasis on[26] "our main doctrines;" nurturing ministries through new organizational structures; and, deploying Christians in the world.

Preaching and Teaching Emphasis on Repentance, Faith, and Holiness

"Our main doctrines, which include all the rest are three—that of repentance, of faith and holiness."[27] Wesley used a vivid metaphor in the presentation of the doctrines when he wrote: repentance (the porch of religion), faith (the door of religion) and holiness (religion itself).

First, repentance (the porch of religion): Repentance is the first step on the road to salvation. Although repentance begins with God's initiative—God's prevenient grace, there is a sense in which repentance calls for a human action or response for wanting and deciding to return to God. For that reason, repentance can also mean "a change of mind or behaviour."[28] John Wesley taught: "Man was created looking directly to God, as his last end; but, falling into sin, he fell off from God, and turned into himself."[29]

The role of prevenient grace is to convict the sinner of his/her sin (John 16:8); to awaken one to his/her senses, like in the parable of the lost son (Luke 15:17), leading the individual towards repentance.[30]

Second, faith (the door of religion): At times faith is known as justifying faith. It is at the door of religion where one experiences justification, to use Wesley's metaphor. Wesley taught that justification had two movements: (a) Preliminary faith or repentance faith, "which includes the free response to God's prevenient grace and a desire to please him but is still only in 'the faith of a servant.'"[31] Wesley describes this level of faith as ". . . its infant state, enables every one that possesses it 'to fear God and work righteousness.'. . . He actually is, at that very moment in a state of acceptance. But he is at present only a servant of God, not properly a son. . . . 'the wrath of God' no longer 'abideth on him.' "[32] (b) Justifying faith "is a sure trust and confidence in Christ bringing a conviction of forgiveness, this being 'the faith of a son.' "[33] For John Wesley, that faith was not merely intellectual understanding and knowledge about the articles of our religion. It meant having "true, Christian, saving faith—a sure trust and confidence to be saved from everlasting damnation, through Christ."[34]

What is justifying faith? Justifying faith describes a very special relationship with God who loves his people in spite of what they have done. It cannot be earned; it is not deserved. It comes freely from God. For example, in the African Shona tradition, a situation may arise, where a parent decides to discipline a child by spanking. A child whose family lives with a grandparent would immediately run away from the angry parent and take refuge with a grandparent, saying: "Ndapotera!" That is, "I have taken refuge in grandma/grandpa." Once the child does this, the wrath of the parent would subside because his/her parent would no longer see just the mischievous child, but also the grandparent. Thus, the parent would withdraw, leaving everything to the grandparent. The state of the child at this point is not that he or she is innocent; rather that he/she is saved from the wrath of the parent by taking refuge in a grandparent. The child's trust in the grandparent would be a saving event. The grandparent would then ask the child: "Tell me, what happened?" Often, the child would feel more comfortable with the grandparent, and tell the truth of what happened, to which the grandparent would often: "Your parent loves you! Don't do it again! Next time be good! I will assure your parent that you are sorry and that next time you will not do it again."

With that assurance from the grandparent, the child could leave his/her grandparent and return to the parent knowing he/she would not be spanked. It does not mean that the child's wrongdoing is condoned; but by admitting his/her wrongdoing to the grandparent, the wrongdoing is momentarily covered (Psalm 32:1). Thus, the child would be justified through faith in the grandparent; or the grandparent would be as Christ to the salvation of the child. John Wesley called this kind of faith, justifying faith—the faith of a child.[35]

In the March 28, 2013 edition of The Upper Room, I shared the conversion story of a woman in a circuit that I pastored. The woman attended church regularly, but she looked withdrawn, sickly, frightened, miserable, and often sat in the back of the church. At a Sunday evening service, she came to kneel at the altar, asking for prayer and healing. Her conversion journey began that evening, and after almost three months of torture and agony, four demonic spirits were cast out of her. At the end of those three months, her whole physical outlook noticeably changed for she began to reflect her inner transformation in the outward aspects of her life. She gained weight, looked radiant and healthy; she actually became herself. One Sunday morning she testified to the whole congregation about her new life:

> Since I committed my life to Christ I have discovered peace in my life. I have discovered new joy and genuine love for my husband and my four children. My life is now filled with new love to serve Christ, my husband, my children, and my church.

She, who once was darkness—even to her family—became light to her family, her church and the community.

Third, holiness (religion itself): John Wesley's scriptural way to salvation, which began with repentance (the porch of religion) and came to faith (the door of religion), ends up entering into holiness (the religion itself). The terms holiness, sanctification, Christian perfection, and love are synonymous. Thus holiness is the love of God appropriated by the Holy Spirit. This is the love that transforms the followers of Christ to be in the likeness of Christ.

Wesley's understanding of the gospel of the grace of God was not limited only to personal piety or to loving God; rather, the gospel of the grace of God also included social holiness—love for your neighbor (Mark 12:31). This is why Wesley and the Wesleyan Revival's focus was on the social issues of their time: ministering to the poor, widows, orphans, and the blind; rejecting the economic necessity of slavery, and all the riches brought in through tears, sweat, and blood of fellow humans; concern for prisoners; and abuse of liquor, which was consumed generously and robbed grain that could feed the poor.[36]

It is this at this last stage on the road toward Christian perfection or of loving God that John Wesley describes as:

> . . . "total resignatio.n to the will of God"—what a modern evangelist might call "complete surrender." But unlike some modern evangelists (and some of his contemporaries also) Wesley does not ask for or expect any such completeness of surrender at the moment of conversion. On the contrary, he believes it rarely, if ever, happens so soon. In fact, . . . with most people it does not happen till they are on their deathbeds; and even when it happens earlier, it often has to happen more than once before it becomes a quite settled state in this life.[37]

I used to have a problem understanding the reference in attaining perfection "on one's death bed," until I heard a legal adviser to the Zimbabwe Annual Conference, of The United Methodist Church explain how wills of individuals are handled; namely that, even if one had written a will, one's last words uttered at his/her deathbed would take priority, because most people would not lie when on their deathbeds.

John Wesley warned his followers that in propounding the doctrine of sanctification, one would not want to encourage enthusiasts of "those who imagine they have the grace which they have not . . . those who imagine they have such gifts from God as they have not . . ." "[38] enthusiasts who imagine themselves to be endowed with powers of working miracles, of healing the sick, prophesy and many others . . . enthusiasts who claim to be guided by God . . . by visions, dreams and strong impressions, or sudden impulses on the mind."[39]

It was in that light of "social holiness" that members of the Wesleyan societies in Britain were able to build up one another in all their endeavors as they related their faith to their personal problems as well as problems caused by social structures. Hence the rules of commitment to the Wesleyan societies that encouraged everyone to continue to evidence their desire for salvation by: (a) by doing no harm to any body and avoiding evil in every kind; (b) by doing good and by being, in every kind, merciful; (c) by attending upon all the ordinances of God—such as public worship, ministry of the word, the Lord's Supper, family and private prayers, searching the scriptures, fasting, and abstinence.[40]

New Organizational Structures for Nurturing Ministries

As much as John Wesley was well known for his autocracy; surprisingly he listened to the fears and aspirations of his converts; and therefore attuned himself to new ideas for the sake of his converts. He forged in new structural groupings that served the purpose of nurturing and guiding the people called Methodists in England[41]—structural organizations that enabled converts to grow toward Christian maturity; or move on from conversion toward Christian perfection. Such structural organizations were: Methodist societies, class meetings, and bands—all for the purpose of what we would call disciple-making today.

First, the establishment of Methodist societies: In 1748 John Wesley made reference to the origin of the Methodist societies, which were established so that Wesley could meet with people to address their concerns and answer their questions. Originally they met in private homes, but as the numbers increased they were able to buy land and build churches.

This space enabled them to meet for public worship; preaching the Word; and administrating the sacraments.

Second, the establishment of class meetings: Wesley developed a ministry of nurturing, a move which brought about another new organizational structure for the Methodists. Wesley's evangelistic ministry differed from those of his contemporaries in that he discovered the importance of caring for his converts. He is quoted as saying, "converts without nurture are like stillborn babies . . . Never encourage the devil by snatching souls from him that you cannot nurture."[42]

As Wesley struggled with how best to care for his converts—to nurture and guide them to Christian maturity—the society in Bristol stumbled on the idea of class meetings. He bought into the idea, which had originated as a way of raising funds for rebuilding a society in Bristol, and eventually developed into a unit of 12 for society membership. Those class meetings became an effective way of transforming people, both personally and in their social relationships, as they met weekly for an hour. It enabled people to work out their quarrels and misunderstanding that often occurred and to learn to bear one another's burdens. Through this process, people began talking to one another in love. Those class meetings provided an opportunity for Bible study and raised the level of Christian education within the people called Methodists, which enabled all the members to grow in Christ.[43]

Third, the deployment of Christians in the world: When it came to the practice of deploying the laity, John Wesley admits that the Wesleyan Revival often "copied after the primitive church."[44] Having been swamped by crowds of the poor, sick and suffering of England, Wesley had no option but to deploy the laity ministry. Lay people were trained and sent to pray, to exhort, teach, and preach in class meetings. They held Bible study; they knew how to preach the gospel of the grace of God in Christ; and they knew what it meant to lead others[45] "in prayer, praise and thanksgiving."[46] These lay people had been class leaders, stewards, and exhorters; and so they were deployed either for local or itinerant ministry. That was the kind of laity Wesley relied on—the laity that sustained the Wesleyan Revival in Britain for over 50 years under Wesley's leadership. No wonder Albert Outler wrote:

> For the greater part of any given year, it was the Methodist laymen who were the most visible exemplars of evangelical Christianity in any given local community; they were the actual sponsors of the Revival, the real martyrs for Christ at the grassroots level.[47]

In sharing the story of the transformation brought by the Bristol Methodist societies through class meetings, John Wesley reported:

> "Kingswood," he told a correspondent in the early winter of 1739, "does not now, as a year ago, resound with cursing and blasphemy. It is no more filled with drunkenness and uncleanness, and the idle diversions that naturally lead thereto. It is no longer full of wars and fighting, of clamour and bitterness, of wrath and envying."[48]

Kingswood was indeed, a changed place, and it was there that John Wesley established a school for the children from poor families, who would have otherwise not received an education.

Summary

The Lord is adding new numbers to his church in Africa on a daily basis and this is a great challenge to the entire Christian community that embraces all versions of Christianity in Africa—Protestant, Roman Catholic, Orthodox, Coptic, African Initiative, and Pentecostal. The challenge that African Christianity faces amidst the evangelization of the continent and the resultant church growth is faithfulness and steadfastness to Christian doctrines, which are founded on the enduring heritage of many past generations. It would seem some of such benchmarks would be the following:

First, evangelization and church growth on the continent of Africa must continue. The work must remain faithful to the biblical witness, namely God's acts culminating in Jesus Christ.

Second, there is need for more creativity in theological reflection and more ways of expressing the Christian faith in Africa contextually. African thinkers today need a theology, which they consider their own, to interpret the Christian faith. There is no way we can advocate and promote the celebration of the risen Christ without doing it as African Christians. It is time to take off the Western religious jacket and put on what is African in our churches.

Third, the Wesleyan method of evangelization teaches us faithfulness to preaching the gospel of grace that, along with other doctrines of the church, emphasizes those doctrines of repentance, faith, and holiness. Above all, the Wesleyan heritage of evangelization teaches us that Christian discipleship is synonymous with growth towards Christian maturity—always pressing "on toward the goal to win the prize for which God has called me [us] heavenward in Christ Jesus" (Philippians 3:14). Evangelism and church growth is not all about numerical growth or counting heads; rather is also about the growth and transformation of the whole person through repentance, faith, and growth to Christian perfection. It was Bishop Nolan Harmon, a late United Methodist, who wrote:

> The doctrine of Christian perfection has been the one specific contribution which Methodism has made to the Church universal.[49]

We have that to offer as we join hands with the rest of other churches on the continent in the task of evangelization and as we witness the daily growth of Christianity.

The Rev. Dr. John Wesley Kurewa is the founding Vice Chancellor of Africa University (AU) and now serves as the E. Stanley Jones Professor of Evangelism at AU. Dr. John Wesley Kurewa, a member of the Zimbabwe Area, is a prolific writer and is dedicated to the vitality of The United Methodist Church in Africa. He is married to Gertrude Rufaro and they have two children and three grandchildren.

2

The Future of Evangelization and Church Growth in Africa

Introduction

The ministry of evangelization and church growth is The United Methodist Church's attempt to implement the mandate of Christ as recorded in Matthew 28:19-20. It is a call upon every believer in Christ to spread the good news of salvation from sin through faith in Jesus Christ.

The United Methodist Church in Africa has been involved in this ministry since its establishment. Statistics have shown the rapid growth of the church in number and in spirit. The church has been involved in various types of ministries in its attempt to reach people with the good news of Jesus by any means possible.

Africa is like what Jesus said in Matthew 9:37: "The harvest is large, but there are few workers to gather it in" (GNT). Evangelization and church growth is a very broad topic, as is the continent of Africa. The continent covers a huge landmass, with an estimated population of about 1.1 billion people. Hence, this chapter focuses primarily on the work of The United Methodist Church in Africa with an emphasis on sub-Saharan Africa.[1]

As the church is planning new strategies for the future, this article will lift up some of the necessary areas that should be of concern to the implementers of the program.

The first section shows the difference between the term evangelism, which is widely used in churches, and evangelization, a more inclusive term. The second section discusses ways to share the good news of Jesus Christ with others. This includes witnessing, winning, nurturing, and building communities. Section three focuses on the whole concept of church growth and includes the numerical, spiritual, and financial perspectives. The next section deals with some prospects for total growth of the church. For example, investment in agriculture and other Christian businesses to help church members increase financial strength; Bible translation to make the Word of God available to people in their native languages; economic transformation to create opportunities to reach more people in their areas of work; increased modern road networks to make remote areas accessible to the carriers of the gospel and the social benefits that accompany it; and modern communication systems all over the continent through the use of cell phones, internet, social media, etc.

The last two sections of the article focus on the challenges the church may encounter in the process and how the church can overcome them. Among the challenges are secularism, corruption, poverty, dual allegiance, and spiritual dryness in the church. To overcome these challenges, the church needs to apply several factors in planning, such as prioritizing evangelization in all the conferences, establishing discipleship training classes in the local churches, making plans to sustain membership growth, and improving places of worship, etc.

The need for courageous leadership is emphasized. There are so many opportunities that are in favor of the good news rather than the opposing forces that are working against the gospel in Africa. The primary need of the church is for visionary and courageous leaders who will lead the way so the members will win the battle against the kingdom of darkness.

Evangelization

Evangelization is a broad concept that involves all that it takes to make the gospel relevant to any group of people anywhere in the world. It is a process and not an event like the word evangelism. As a process, it includes:

> Witnessing: Sharing with another person the gospel message of salvation through faith in Jesus Christ, backed by one's personal testimony of how one received eternal life. A true witness must know the gospel story of Christ's birth, life, ministry, mission on earth, suffering, death, and resurrection, sending of the Holy Spirit, and planting of the Church.
>
> Deciding: When the listener understands and accepts the truth of the gospel is the moment of decision. The person's decision to turn away from sin and towards Christ is sealed by the church through water baptism (e.g., Acts 8:34-39).
>
> Nurturing/Discipleship: After the decision to accept the gospel and turn away from all sinful habits is made, the person becomes a child in the things of God. New believers must be mentored by mature believers by teaching the truth of God's Word, the work of the Holy Spirit in their life, and the necessity of worshiping God, witnessing to the truth and reality of salvation, prayer, and fellowshipping with other believers, and giving to the work of the church.

Now is the time for congregations and their leaders to be practical as they implement their evangelization program. They must produce materials that are easily read and understood by committed members in sharing the good news with others. The members must be taught how to present the good news in a conversational and logical manner that will convince listeners that the gospel is worth accepting and believing. The nurturing process begins when the person accepts the gospel and decides to become a follower of Jesus Christ.

The United Methodist Church has a solid foundation to build up congregations for the spiritual and numerical growth of its members. That foundation is the method used by John Wesley and his team. Wesley's plan was to nurture new converts for Christian maturity. He organized the converts into classes, societies, and bands, giving each member an opportunity to actively participate in Bible study, praying for others, sharing experiences with others, confessing to one another, and exercising self-control, which is the fruit of the Holy Spirit. The church must revisit that plan, refine it where necessary, and use it to make disciples for Christ. Wesley's documents are still obtainable from the General Board of Discipleship of The United Methodist Church and other libraries. The church must study Paul's blueprint laid out in his letters to Timothy and the Ephesians. Paul wrote to Timothy:

> You then, my child, be strong in the grace that is in Christ Jesus; and what you have heard from me through many witnesses entrust to faithful people who will be able to teach others as well. (2 Timothy 2:1-2, NIV)

That is multiplication evangelism.

Paul wrote to the church in Ephesus instructing them of the responsibility of gifted leaders in the church:

> It was he (Christ) who "gave gifts to people"; he appointed some to be apostles, others to be prophets, others to be evangelists, and others to be pastors and teachers. He did this to prepare all God's people for the work of Christian service, in order to build up the body of Christ. (Ephesians 4:11-12, GNT)

The gospel must not only be taught or listened to; it must also be practiced and shared with others that they too may be saved by its power through faith in Jesus Christ, the Son of God. Leaders must demonstrate before the new converts how to present the gospel in a conversational manner. Members must be taught how to share their faith with others until faith sharing or witnessing for Christ becomes a lifestyle for them.

One of the success stories expected to come out of the evangelization and church growth movement is the strengthening of existing churches and planting of new ones.

I remember a story I heard in Ghana when I attended a seminar on evangelism. The author of the story was not mentioned. Here is the story:

Now it came to pass that a group existed who called themselves fishermen. And lo, there were many fish in the waters all around. In fact the whole area was surrounded by streams and lakes filled with fish. And the fish were hungry.

Week after week, month after month, and year after year, those who called themselves fishermen met in meetings and talked about their call to fish, the abundance of fish, and how they might go about fishing. Year after year, they carefully defined what fishing means, defended fishing as an occupation, and declared that fishing is always to be a primary task of fishermen.

These fishermen built large, beautiful buildings called "Fishing Headquarters." The plea was that everyone should be a fisherman and every fisherman should fish. One thing they did not do, however, was fish.

In addition to meeting regularly, they organized societies to send out fishermen to other places where there were many fish. These societies were formed by those who had the great vision and courage to speak about fishing, to define fishing, and to promote the idea of fishing in far away streams and lakes where many other fish of different colors lived.

Large, elaborate, and expensive training centers were built with the original and primary purpose to teach fishermen how to fish. Over the years, courses were offered on the needs of fish, the nature of fish, where to find fish, the psychological reactions of fish, and how to approach and feed fish. Those who taught had doctorates in fishology. But the teachers did not fish. They only taught fishing.

After one stirring meeting on The Necessity of Fishing, one young fellow left the meeting and went fishing. The next day he reported he had caught two outstanding fish. He was honored for his excellent catch and scheduled to visit all the big meetings possible to tell how he did it. So he quit his fishing in order to have time to tell about his experience to the other fishermen. He was also placed on the Fishermen's General Board as a person having considerable experience.

Imagine how hurt some were when one day a person suggested that those who don't catch fish were really not fishermen, no matter how much they claimed to be. Yet it did sound correct. Is a person a fisherman if year after year he never catches a fish? Jesus said, "Follow me, and I will make you fishers of men."[2]

Every member of the church from top to bottom must evangelize and not just organize seminars and workshops on evangelization and church growth in Africa. Members should be equipped with such practical lessons that include, among other things, topical Bible study, mobilizing the church for multiplication evangelization, how to deal with sin, God's plan of salvation, work of the Holy Spirit in evangelization, etc.

Building Communities

For a vibrant future, the leaders of The United Methodist Church in Africa must consider the mission of the denomination to be inspiring a new vision for local ministries, empowering, and equipping members of the local churches to minister to the whole person. It should not be just of preparing people for heaven. This is exactly what the apostles did immediately after the Day of Pentecost. They formed a community of believers with a clear mental picture of God's worldview. Acts 4:32 states that "The group of believers was one in mind and heart. None of them said that any of their belongings were their own; but they all shared with one another everything they had" (GNT).

There have been times when we see new converts leaving everything they have to follow Christ through the church. The lives of some were threatened either by the group they were abandoning or by their family members who felt betrayed. The Church is God's kingdom community within the world's community (John 17:6-16; cf. Ephesians 4:1-16). A teacher once said, "The early church was built on the basis of a caring community." It is important that church leaders know this truth and act upon it. It is a well-organized and caring community that will encourage new converts to remain in the church as the body of Christ (Acts 6:1-7).

The church must revisit its mission on the continent, and set new goals and objectives that will guide its activities in the quest to capture Africa for the kingdom of God. It is the Spirit-filled community life of a church that usually inspires members to assume responsibilities and work for the health and total growth of the congregation. When a church is functioning as a spiritual community, its members see their services as a blessing rather than a burden. They give a portion of their resources willingly and not grudgingly to spread the gospel of Jesus Christ to the end of the world.

Evangelism, on the other hand, is an event that people do within a set time frame such as a revival, crusade, street preaching, workshops and seminars, literature distribution, and so forth. Many times revivals and crusades are conducted without serious follow-up for the purpose of identifying the new converts and enlisting them in the congregation for discipleship training. I have seen people preaching in the street without any connection with an established congregation. Then I ask myself, what becomes of the people who accept the gospel and want to be a part of the body of Christ? I believe that such individuals go back to their sinful ways of living and make the Christian faith a mockery among others living around them. That is why I think it is very important for evangelism and evangelization to work hand-in-hand for the complete salvation of people from the world of sin and into God's family of loving and caring people.

Courageous Leadership

For The United Methodist Church in Africa to fulfill its future plans, the denomination must encourage and promote courageous leadership. It needs leaders that will demonstrate courage as the church faces strong opposition from anti-Christ groups in the spiritual, political, and social arenas of society. Our world is full of confused people who eagerly spread their confusing ideas. Some of them argue that the Bible contains errors and contradictions while others speak of the resurrection of Christ as a myth. As a result, such persons reject the lordship of Jesus Christ.

The church needs leaders who will not compromise the truth of the gospel for any kind of benefit; who will depend on the power of the Holy Spirit; who will rally believers and use their spiritual gifts to help people who are far from God to become fully devoted followers of Jesus Christ. We need leaders who will lead by example. The church in Africa needs courageous leaders because of the forces of evil that believers are encountering daily (mentioned above). Such leaders must be men and women who are walking daily with Jesus Christ. We need leaders who will evaluate the past activities of a church in order to courageously chart new and achievable goals and objectives for the future based upon their God-given vision. Such visionary planning will enable the church to avoid the errors of the past.

Those that will lead The United Methodist Church in Africa must be spiritually and intellectually mature. The United Methodist Church in Africa needs leaders that will not compromise the truth of the gospel, but who will inspire the church to stand for justice and freedom on the continent. False teachers are undermining the faith of believers. They are leading a lot of people astray.

Today, the business climate in Africa is attracting many Asian nationals with their various religious beliefs and practices. They are convincing Africans to believe that their gods can give people instant wealth, prosperity, and promotion. As a result, many people are surrendering to those false gods for prosperity and political power. We need leaders who, through the power of the Holy Spirit, will open the eyes of the people they minister to, so they will see the danger of such erroneous teachings.

George Liddell gave five reasons why good leadership is important in the church (especially in Africa) as follows:

1. Leaders make or break an organization.
2. Leaders advance or destroy a cause.
3. Leaders inspire or frustrate a mission.
4. Leaders motivate and mobilize or stagnate and demoralize a movement.
5. Leaders lead the way or lose the way.[3]

John Maxwell, commenting on some qualities of King Josiah's leadership in 2 Chronicles 34:3-33, wrote: "As the leader goes, so go the people—for good or for evil."[4] John Maxwell's conclusion can be compared to what Christ said in Matthew 15:14, "when one blind man leads another, they both fall into the ditch" (GNT).

The Church needs leaders in Africa who can inspire dedicated believers to pursue the spiritual and physical needs of the people. They must be Spirit-filled men and women who are capable of setting achievable goals and objectives; and prioritizing the implementation of those goals and objectives in order to accomplish the purpose of evangelization and church growth in Africa.

I stress the importance of evangelization as compared to evangelism because in the evangelization process, a church identifies and works to meet the basic social and spiritual needs of the people it wants to convert and disciple for the kingdom of God. The God-given vision of the church is fulfilled when it gets involved in meeting the physical, spiritual, mental, and social needs of people. It is in the evangelization process that the church reaches the point of building institutions like schools, clinics, hospitals, agricultural projects, leadership development, and other aspects of caring ministries.

Evangelization, then, is a ministry without end. As such, it requires the full participation of every United Methodist regardless of tribe, education, wealth, position, or affluence. Members must be guided through teaching, preaching, and prayer. They must be led to understand how to set goals and objectives as they mature in the faith and begin to take initiatives to better render services to humanity. An annual strategic plan would help the church in this process.

Scripture tells how Jesus Christ went everywhere preaching, teaching, healing the sick, feeding the hungry, casting out demons, and bringing the dead to life again (Matthew 9:35-38). That is evangelization. A colleague of mine in ministry once said to me that, "The mission of God is not just about getting people saved but it is about doing what is right in the sight of God." His statement supports what we read in Matthew 7:21 when Christ said:

> "It is not everyone who calls me 'Lord, Lord,' will enter the Kingdom of heaven, but only those who do what my Father wants them to do." (GNT)

I believe that it was this kind of thinking that guided the participants at the consultative meeting held in Nairobi, Kenya in 2000 to agree to adopt the strategic goal called academies with the aim of conducting train-the-trainers teaching sections in the various African regions where The United Methodist Church is present and working. Participating members of the conferences at the academies were to be intellectually equipped and spiritually empowered to replicate the knowledge gained in order to enable an entire congregation to multiply the knowledge and methods by training others in their respective congregations. A similar method was used by Jesus Christ and the apostle Paul (Luke 10:1, ff. 2 Timothy 2:1-2).

The academies that were conducted in the past were rewarding in many ways. But I noticed three factors as being responsible for the academies not producing the desired results. (1) The academies lacked a practical approach. The presentations were more intellectual than practical. As a result, some members of the church observed that no replications were reported at conference sessions. (2) The participants failed to implement what they learned from the academies. (3) Conference leadership was unprepared to place evangelization as a number-one priority in their annual plans. We need to learn from the weaknesses of the academies to avoid these same issues in the future.

The Holy Spirit in Evangelization and Church Growth

The New Testament stresses the importance of the work of the Holy Spirit in the lives of believers. It is the Holy Spirit who gives God's vision to leaders (Acts 13:1-3) and defines God's mission for the church (Acts 1:4-8). Hence, it is important that leaders are filled with the Holy Spirit (Ephesians 5:18). I hope that all leaders who accept appointment in The United Methodist Church for the evangelization of Africa and the growth of the church will be Holy Spirit-filled and walk in the truth of God's Word. They must yield their personal agenda to the leadership of the Holy Spirit. They must learn from the apostle Paul. When Paul received God's vision for the Gentiles (Acts 9:15; 22:21), he altered his personal agenda. This is what Paul wrote to the elders in Ephesus:

But I do not count my life of any value nor as precious to myself, if only I may finish my course and the ministry that I received from the Lord Jesus. (Acts 20:24, GNT)

Paul's ultimate priority in his ministry was to fulfill the vision that Christ had given him. God has a vision for the transformation of Africa. But regrettably, so many of the leaders have not owned the vision. As a result, the God-given vision dies in many churches on the continent, and God's people are perishing for lack of knowledge (Hosea 4:6). Evangelization in Africa needs leaders who will own the God-given vision for the transformation of Africa and take responsibility for its achievement. They must endeavor to inspire others who will assist them in the implementation process (Acts 11:25; 18:24-28). Churches will not grow as expected if their leaders are not guided and influenced by the presence of the Holy Spirit in their work.

Paul met about 12 men in Ephesus and asked them, "'Did you receive the Holy Spirit when you became believers?' 'We have not even heard that there is a Holy Spirit,' they answered" (Acts 19:1-2 GNT). Later in the passage Paul explained to them the difference between the baptism of John the Baptist and that of Jesus Christ, and they agreed to be baptized in the name of Jesus Christ (vv. 3-5). Paul baptized them in the name of Jesus Christ, laid his hands on them, and prayed, and 12 men then received the Holy Spirit. The most interesting part of the story is that when Paul's preaching and teaching were rejected in the synagogue, he withdrew from there and went in the lecture hall of Tyrannus with the believers. After two years, "all the people who lived in the province of Asia, both Jews and Gentiles, heard the word of the Lord" (v. 10, GNT). That is how the gospel is spread and the church grows when Spirit-filled leaders lead it.

Church Growth

The growth of the church must be viewed from three major dimensions: numerical, spiritual, and financial.

Numerical Growth

Churches grow numerically from two angles, biological and spiritual multiplication. Biologically, people become members of congregations through birth and marriage. Some people join congregations when they decide to follow their spouses to become members of the spouse's congregation. Other people claim church membership because their parents are members of the congregation or denomination. Church leadership must be willing to recognize such members and assimilate them into the membership of the church and enlist them into discipleship classes in the church.

Spiritual Growth

Normally spiritual growth results from evangelization when people hear the gospel, repent, and are baptized by the Holy Spirit after they are baptized in water. Conversion is the work of the Holy Spirit. Sharing the good news is the work of the believer. So, spiritual growth is a combination of what the believer and the Holy Spirit do together. In the end, more people are added to the number of believers in a local church and the denomination (Acts 5:14). However, all members must be nurtured until they become mature, growing believers in the body of Christ (see Ephesians 4:11-16). It is the power of the Holy Spirit that takes away weaknesses such as timidity, shyness, fear, stubbornness, and disobedience to the truth of God's Word, and fills them with courage, boldness to witness to the truth, compassion, humility, honesty, and the power to conquer all temptations to sin against God. Therefore, it is important for all leaders and followers in the church to take seriously the admonition that Christ gave to the apostles: "Do not leave Jerusalem, but wait for the gift I told you about . . . when the Holy Spirit comes upon you, you will be filled with power, and you will be witnesses for me . . ." (Acts 1:4, 8; GNT).

I experienced this type of church growth in 1983 when I was appointed by my bishop, Bishop Arthur F. Kulah, to the Firestone Rubber Plantation in Liberia to serve as the religious affairs director. The pastor I succeeded served in that capacity for 10 successive years. When I took over the office,

I learned that there were less than 20 organized churches on the plantation. Out of a total work force of about 20,000 employees, only about 3,000 employees were active Christians. I could not tell the number of inactive members. Many of the inactive members, as they were introduced to me, were holding managerial and executive secretary positions. I conducted a series of interviews and I discovered that there had not been a practice of intentional evangelization and well-organized discipleship-training classes conducted by the pastors in the local churches. Another cause of the low active membership was the assumption of some pastors that the employees were too busy with their jobs and they did not have the time for Bible studies, prayer services, and outreach.

We organized Bible study classes, prayer services, telephone evangelism, youth ministry, and visitation teams. At the end of three months, we planned a five-day revival to which we invited some spirit-filled pastors from different churches to preach and teach. At the end of the revival, about 102 converts (96 adult men and women and six young adults) were baptized at one time. One month later, I left the plantation to study at Asbury Theological Seminary in Wilmore, Kentucky, USA. Before the end of the following month, I received a report that Mr. George Warner, one of the young adults who was baptized with the 102 candidates, shared the gospel message on his school campus daily. The Holy Spirit blessed his effort by converting 400 students and nine teachers, seven of whom were Muslims. This is a testimony to the fact that there is still a great hunger and thirst for the gospel in Africa. The harvest in Africa is large. The laborers are few. But the leaders of the church are not making sufficient efforts to hire potential workers for the Lord's harvest.

As the church is preparing for its future growth, it must focus on recruiting potential believers and equipping them so that they will go out on the field to win more followers and bring them into the body of Christ.

Financial Growth

The third level of growth that The United Methodist Church in Africa needs to promote and encourage is financial growth. The church needs to work hard so that it can become financially independent and self-supporting. The church has been depending on outside support for its ministries for a long time. If the church in Africa is to accomplish its God-given vision and mission, it must start training its members to support the ministries without waiting for money from New York, Germany, Norway, or Sweden. The concept of stewardship and accountability must be taught in every congregation in more realistic ways.

Accountability is a very important area for consideration in the growth process of the church. Church leaders and members must be held accountable for all the resources entrusted to them to support the ministries and the institutions that are operated by the church. Church accounts must be audited periodically for proper accountability. Church members must practice honesty at all times and in all business transactions. If The United Methodist Church in Africa is to become financially independent in the future, its members must be disciplined when found involved in corrupt practices anywhere, whether in government, in the church, in business, or in private life. There are many wealthy Christians in Africa and the world. Many of them are willing to give regularly to the church. But when they hear about mismanagement and corruption in the church, they usually withdraw their support because no one wants to continue supporting an organization whose leadership cannot be trusted, and where transparency is not practiced.

Despite reports of high numerical growth of The United Methodist Church in Africa, there is still room for new believers to come to the Lord. Africa has many unreached people groups, which have been neglected by pastors and members of the church. The groups can be found in cities, towns, villages, concession areas, and industrial camps. Some of them are found in nightclubs and video clubs in every city in Africa. But our churches are not making enough effort to reach them and share the gospel with them.

In the 1980s, a colleague and I were discussing the idea of planning an evangelistic strategy that we could use to capture parts of Monrovia, the capital city of Liberia, within a couple of months. We started listing people groups in the city. We noticed that churches were not paying attention to them at that time. Among them were employees of our diplomatic missions, immigrants from other African countries, and business people who are Indian, Lebanese, Syrian, Fula, as well as fishermen from Ghana and Togo.

We recruited a few young men to help us do a survey of the groups we identified and we were amazed at the number of persons living near the church, but were not reached with the gospel on a regular basis. It reminded me of the story Jesus told in Matthew 20:1-16: "The kingdom of heaven is like the landowner who went out early in the morning to hire laborers for his vineyard. . . . And about five o'clock he went out and found others standing around; and he said to them, 'Why are you standing here idle all day?' "7 They said to him, 'Because no one has hired us' " [emphasis added]. Churches are built in similar situations. There are potential Christians, but no one from the nearby churches has bothered to reach them with the gospel and invite them to meet Jesus Christ.

As a result of that exercise, my friend and I decided to select and train members of our two congregations to share the gospel with people in the groups mentioned above. We started making friends with foreign nationals in some of the embassies near Monrovia. Our friends were in the USA, Ghana, Nigeria, and Sierra Leone embassies. As a result, people from those embassies began to attend our worship services and rendered outstanding support to the ministries.

Another wonderful experience I had was with a Muslim fellow. At first I did not know that he was a Muslim. I decided to go to visit him one afternoon. While we were conversing on his little porch, the Muslim call to prayer was made. He begged me to wait because the prayer would be short. When he returned, I asked him whether he understood the Arabic I heard the prayer leader speaking. He said, "No." So I asked why he went there since he could not understand Arabic. This is what he said:

Why can't I go there when you Christians don't have time for us? We are living in this town. Many times Christians passed by this town in their cars singing on their way to other towns. No Christian group has ever stopped to speak to us about Jesus Christ. That is why when some Muslims came and started telling us about God, we decided to join them. Later, they built this small Mosque in our town for us to worship.

This sounds like what the men told the farmer in the parable in Matthew 20:6, when they said: "No one hired us." The man and the people of that village were not against the gospel; neither did they reject the message. But no Christian had witnessed to them.

For evangelization and church growth to be successful in the future, congregations must be equipped and guided in the basic ways in which churches grow.

Despite all the corruption reports being published from Africa, there are so many ways in which The United Methodist Church in Africa can become spiritually and financially independent. Among them are the following:

Investment Opportunities in Agriculture

Though people regard Africa as a poor continent, Africa is not as poor as people think. Chika Onyeani is quoted in The African Sun Times, stating, "Africa continues to be demonized as the poorest continent in the world, yet it is the richest continent in terms of its natural resources."[5] For example:

- Agriculture. It has been said that Zambia, Zimbabwe, and the Democratic Republic of Congo have the agricultural potential to feed the entire continent. It is also true of my country, Liberia. The country has the agricultural potential to feed its population plus many more people in the sub-region. If the church would invest in agriculture and encourage its members to go back to the soil, the church would experience an unprecedented financial growth to support and sustain all of its ministries. Evangelization and church growth programs in Africa would no longer be a burden to anyone. It would be a joy to share the faith with practical examples that strengthen the message.
- Water. Africa is home to some of the greatest rivers in the world, e.g., the Nile, Congo, Niger, and Zambezi rivers. The Nile River has a basin that covers 10 percent of the continent. Liberia has more access to water than many countries in Africa. As close as Liberia is to the equator, I have never experienced or heard about Liberia experiencing drought for more than 165 years. Liberia has many rivers and creeks plus abundant annual rainfall to enable the citizens to grow food and cash crops to sustain financial growth. Some of the rivers and lakes have wonderful sites for tourism. Tourism can provide substantial income for local people, as well as for the government, which will enable church members to contribute meaningfully to the financial needs of the church.
- Energy. Africa has virtually unlimited energy potential. The continent has 40 percent of the world's hydroelectric potential. Besides hydroelectric energy, many countries in Africa can invest in solar energy that will benefit both urban and rural citizens. Currently, the Liberian government is investing in a solar power lighting system to provide traffic lights in Monrovia.

Modern Road Networks

Many nations in Africa are making frantic efforts to build good modern road networks for transporting goods and services from one country to another. Quite recently, leaders of the four countries in the Mano River Basin in West Africa (Liberia, Sierra Leone, Guinea, and Côte d Ivoire) met and agreed that each government must improve a portion of the road that connects it to the other countries. The completion of such a project will certainly enhance the dissemination of the gospel to every people group in the sub-region.

Bible Translation

Another thing that God is doing to spread the gospel among the various ethnic groups in Africa is the translation of the Bible in as many local languages as possible on the continent. Many Christian denominations and NGOs are training and employing the services of committed for literacy work among the local people of the continent. There is evidence of the people's hunger and thirst after God's Word, especially when it can be read in their own language.

Economic Transformation

There are some countries in Africa that are experiencing economic growth.

Looking at the picture just painted about the economic potential of the continent, the church can become financially independent with effective and efficient leadership that will dialogue with their respective governments regarding investments that will strengthen the economy of the countries. The church in Africa that is striving for financial independence and to become self-supporting needs to work hard to encourage its members to invest their time, finances, and energy in meaningful ways. Its members need to produce more than what they consume, rather than just consuming more than what they produce. It is clearly stated in scripture that if we seek first the kingdom of God and his righteousness, all other things will be given to us (Matthew 6:33).

We are not to just teach people how to preach the gospel, but also how to make a living for themselves and help others as well (Ephesians 4:28). Our Lord demonstrated to his followers the inappropriateness of sending people home hungry after preaching to them for hours. Find something for them to eat (Matthew 14:16).

Another important factor to be considered is training members to recognize the principle of combining personal piety with social responsibility. United Methodist leaders and members need to learn from Christ and adopt his evangelization strategy. Christ did not revolt against civil authorities; neither did he succumb to them. He encouraged his disciples to pay their taxes (Matthew 17:22-27). Church members should not refuse to contribute to meaningful community projects in the name of poverty. When it comes to giving financial support to community projects, we hear Christians saying, "Where do we get the money? We are struggling to make ends meet." We must take the advice of Paul to the Thessalonians. He wrote to them in 1 Thessalonians 4:11-12:

Make it your aim to live a quiet life, to mind your own business, and to earn your own living, just as we told you before. In this way you will win the respect of those who are not believers, and you will not have to depend on anyone for what you need. (GNT)

The church must not spoon-feed the members by always giving them money, food, clothes, and medications for free. Instead, the church must encourage its members to do honest work, teach them the value of work, like Paul and others did in Thessalonica and other towns (2 Thessalonians 3:6-9). Training, equipping, sending out, and supporting members of local churches are some ways by which the church can fulfill the task assigned to it by our Lord. Church members are to respect civil authorities and contribute to the national developmental agenda. When church members perform humble duties out of love and respect for the people among whom they live, they build bridges for evangelization and the fruit of the gospel will be seen. For example:

1. Broken relationships will be mended.
2. Hopes will be restored.
3. Violence will be reduced or eradicated.
4. Spiritual growth will be experienced.

Church members must demonstrate the metaphor Jesus used in the Sermon on the Mount when he said:

"You are the salt of the earth . . . You are the light of the world" (Matthew 5:13-14, GNT). The church is under obligation to demonstrate the fruit of the gospel throughout the world as a witness to all people that the gospel has the power to change lives and physical circumstances. This is done not only by what believers preach, but also by how they live among unbelievers according to God's standard in scripture.

The late Bishop S. Trowen Nagbe of the Liberia Annual Conference once said that, "If you do not know your enemy, you end up fighting against your friend." All national United Methodist leaders operating in Africa must learn the potential challenges of the gospel as well as the opportunities and prospects so they can determine the kind of strategy the church needs to overcome them and sow the seed of the gospel even in hostile communities.

Challenges

Despite numerous challenges and setbacks, the denomination has made significant strides in spreading the gospel to many sub-Saharan countries. Among the challenges the church in Africa faces today are political persuasions, desire for social prestige, generational gaps, greed for power and money, corruption in high and low places, homosexuality, and alcoholism. Usually it is at the local level that a church encounters these challenges. Therefore, the first major challenge a church needs to address is training and appointing evangelistically minded and Spirit-filled local leaders who will take evangelization and church growth into the future work of the Church in Africa. Conferences need to give more attention and resources to members of the local church. The strength of every conference depends on the strength of the congregations. If a congregation is weak and spiritually dead, the conference will be in the same condition.

The local church is God's primary agency for accomplishing God's divine purpose of transforming individuals, communities, regions, and nations. It is the ground for the spiritual warfare that is taking place in every country. If members of the local church are well equipped and empowered with knowledge, skills, and finances to combat the challenging forces of Satan, new churches will be planted and more territories will be captured for the kingdom of God.

As the denomination grows, so will the problems people encounter. Therefore, in addition to leadership development, I have chosen to highlight a few of the numerous challenges facing the work of the church in Africa. For the church to be able to overcome these and maintain relevance and credibility of the gospel, its members must be motivated and inspired to stand up for the truth of the gospel. Hence, it is important at this time that the church carefully plan for the future benefit of evangelization and church growth in Africa in the face of the numerous challenges.

Some of the challenges that are battling against the planting of the gospel in the hearts and lives of the people include the following:

Secularism

This term simply means living a nonreligious lifestyle that is described in the Bible as a worldly lifestyle. Secularism is prevalent in places where people claim human rights and freedom of speech. As a result, both young and old persons are seen getting involved in all kinds of social activities that they regard to be their human rights. They claim that nobody can stop them from living their lives the way they want to live.[6]

While it may be true that no human being can stop them, we believe that the gospel of Jesus Christ can not only stop a sinner from living in sin, but also has the power to transform sinners into saints and make them better citizens of the countries to which they belong. Saving people from the wrath of God and preparing them for good citizenship in this world is one of the goals for the evangelization of Africa.

Corruption

Another important enemy of financial growth and godly character development on both the local and national levels is corruption. Keith Richburg's opinions on corruption in Africa from his book, Out of America: A Black Man Confronts Africa, are discussed in Against All Hope: Hope for Africa by Darrow L. Miller with Scott Allen. Miller and Allen note that, "Not all corruption is equal. Richburg makes a distinction between 'productive corruption' and 'malignant corruption.' "[7]

Miller and Allen illustrate the point with this story: "In Indonesia, the President's daughter might get the contract to build the toll roads . . . but the roads do get built and they do facilitate traffic flow. In Africa, the roads never get built. This is the difference between productive corruption and malignant corruption."[8] Corruption is destroying the fabric of life wherever it is practiced in the world. It damages good systems of leadership in the world. Corruption also occurs in portions of the church. As the light of Christ in the world, the church must discipline its members when they are found guilty of corrupt practices in their daily activities.

Poverty

The problem of poverty is a major issue that no human organization should fail to address. Several individuals and groups have tried to find the cause or causes of poverty. Some blame it on governments, others on multinational companies, while others blame it on the global economic system.

No wonder when Jesus was accused of not providing a means for them to take care of the poor, he told his critics, "You will always have poor people with you, but you will not always have me" (John 12:8, GNT).

The church need not wait to know the cause or causes of poverty before it helps its members to live above abject poverty. God told Adam, "Because of what you have done, the ground will be under a curse. You will have to work hard all your life to make it produce enough food for you" (Genesis 3:17, GNT). Church leaders should not allow their members to hide behind the notion that that they can do nothing to help either the church or themselves because they are poor. They need to be encouraged to learn skills and find ways in which they can earn a living. They should not be encouraged to depend on gifts from abroad. Let members of the church learn from the advice Paul gave the church in Ephesus. "If you used to rob, you must stop robbing and start working, in order to earn an honest living for yourself and to be able to help the poor" (Ephesians 4:28, GNT).

The church can address the issue of poverty among its members by involving them in skill-training sessions and encouraging them to use those skills appropriately for their benefit. The church can also teach the members some financial management techniques that may save them from unnecessary debt. Budgeting is a helpful tool for the church, individual members, and families. When members practice good financial management, there will be great improvement in the places of worship and the livelihood of church members.

Dual Allegiance

In an article concerning the attitude of some Christians, Abram Kidd, a missionary serving in Northwestern Tanzania wrote: "Of all the challenges facing the church, particularly in rural Africa, dual allegiance is perhaps the largest. The health of the church may be gauged by how it handles this issue." He concluded the issue by quoting Jesus' words in Matthew 6:24: "No one can serve two masters."[9]

I see many United Methodists pledging dual allegiance where I live. They divide their allegiance for several reasons: social prestige, political power, promotion on the job, favoritism, spiritual insurance, etc. Many of them do this when seeking alternative sources for power, protection, and wealth. Many people in my country practice dual allegiance because of their experience with African Traditional Religion (ATR). It is widely accepted by the traditionalists that "religion is a way of life." So they see nothing wrong with bringing together a little bit of Christianity, Masonic Craft, ATR, and Western civilization in a religious system they think to be Christianity. This is what is called syncretism.

Another contributing factor to the practice of dual allegiance is the fear of witchcraft that is prevalent in Africa. Many people still attribute their failure or success to the power of witchcraft, so they may go to church and then from there go consult an oracle for a solution to their problems.

Leaders of the church must endeavor to provide the appropriate guidance, biblical teaching, and preaching to help the members see the error in paying dual allegiance. When leaders of the church are found practicing syncretism, other members find comfort in doing the same. The success of evangelization and church growth in Africa depends partly on how members practice the Christian faith. It is not the quantity (church membership) that counts, but the quality (faithfulness and obedience) of our faith.

Spiritual Dryness

Spiritual dryness is a spiritual condition that kills the vision and mission of the church in which it exists. It is one of the contributing factors for the practice of dual allegiance among believers in Africa.

The Church of Jesus Christ cannot win worldly people into the kingdom of God without the empowerment of the Holy Spirit. The life and ministry of John Wesley is a great testimony to the fact of this conviction. The church needs the power and wisdom of the Holy Spirit to effectively implement its mission to the world. It is not an option for the leaders and members of the church to be baptized in the Holy Spirit. One of the first statements the resurrected Christ made to the disciples was, "Receive the Holy Spirit" (John 20:22, GNT). He did not say, "Please receive the Holy Spirit" or "If you want to" or "You may receive the Holy Spirit." He emphatically said, "Receive the Holy Spirit." Receiving the Holy Spirit is a mandate for all believers who are willing and ready to leave all, take up their cross, and follow Christ Jesus.

In one of his messages to the believers in Rome, the apostle Paul said, "Whoever does not have the Spirit of Christ does not belong to him" (Romans 8:9, GNT). So, if The United Methodist Church is expecting to fulfill its God-given vision and mission to evangelize the continent of Africa, its leaders and members appointed to that mission must seek diligently to be filled with the power and wisdom of the Spirit of Christ. Paul advised the believers in Ephesus "not to get drunk with wine, which will only ruin you; instead, be filled with the Spirit" (Ephesians 5:18, GNT). Only the Holy Spirit can renew the hearts and minds of people and give people the ability to understand the good and perfect will of God (Romans 12). Theological education without the Holy Spirit's empowerment is like a sharp kitchen knife without a handle. Theological education without spiritual empowerment is inadequate for the battle against sin and Satan. Fear of witchcraft, as mentioned above, is still a powerful force in Africa that is tempting people on the continent to turn to other supplementary spiritual powers for defense and security. Therefore, victory for the church over all the forces of darkness is possible only through the leadership and empowerment of the Spirit of Christ.

Let the church remember what Paul wrote about this situation:

> Finally, build up your strength in union with the Lord and by means of his mighty power. Put on all the armor that God gives you, so that you will be able to stand up against the Devil's evil tricks. For we are not fighting against human beings, but against the wicked spiritual forces in the heavenly world, the rulers, authorities, and cosmic powers of this dark age. So put on God's armor now! Then when the evil day comes, you will be able to resist the enemy's attacks; and after fighting to the end, you will still hold your ground.
>
> So stand ready, with truth as a belt tight around your waist, with righteousness as your breastplate, and as your shoes the readiness to announce the Good News of peace. At all times carry faith as a shield; for with it you will be able to put out the entire burning arrow shot by the Evil One. And accept salvation as a helmet, and the word of God as the sword which the Spirit gives you. Do all this in prayer . . . (Ephesians 6:10-18, GNT)

In this passage, Paul has provided for the church all that it needs to overcome the problem of spiritual dryness in any congregation.

Overcoming spiritual dryness in a congregation requires obedience to the Word of God, standing firmly on the truth of God's Word, and faith in Jesus Christ.

Prospects

Despite the many challenges facing the church, there is a bright future for its growth. Spiritually, God is raising up many single-minded Christians and congregations that are filled with the power of the Holy Spirit and are proclaiming the gospel in the name of Jesus Christ all over the continent. Currently, there is a group of people who commit themselves to praying for God to send a revival upon the land. They call themselves Christo-Schenon and they have successfully formed groups in all 15 counties of Liberia. Their task is to pray for God to send revival to transform the country.

Another thing that God is doing for the advancement of the gospel is the translation of the Bible in many African languages. People all over the continent are hungry and thirsty for God's Word. They are ready for the harvest. They simply need the committed people to bring them into the fellowship of God's family and nurture them.

The continent is opening up for a great economic transformation through modern road networks, communication networks, political stability, and social justice. The continent is now sending out missionaries to other countries as it did in the beginning. Our hope is built on the promises of Christ, who said, "I will be with you always, to the end of the age" (Matthew 28:20, GNT). Christ has opened doors in the remotest parts of Africa for the spreading of the gospel just as he said in Revelation 3:7. Though the laborers are few at the moment, the harvest is truly ripe. If The United Methodist Church will send equipped and empowered laborers into the vineyard, there will be great rejoicing in the future. Let us act now!

Overcoming the Challenges

The challenges before the church are numerous, and should not be overlooked. At the same time, we need not be afraid because greater is the power that is in us than the power that is in the world (1 John 4:4). All the church needs to do for great victories is adequate preparation of the mind, spirit, body, and emotion of its members. Let the church put in place the following steps:

- Prioritize evangelization in all the conferences.
- Establish discipleship-training classes in all the congregations.
- Work to achieve financial independence.
- Plan to sustain membership growth.
- Develop strategies for rural and urban ministries.
- Involve every small group in the evangelization movement.
- Plan to improve places of worship for all congregations.
- Organize adult literacy classes for illiterate members.
- Mobilize the congregations in prayer.
- Let every member know the importance of blending personal piety and social responsibility for community development.

Conclusion

The vision for the evangelization and church growth in Africa is exciting. There are so many opportunities in favor of the church as compared to the opposing forces that are trying to work against the church.

Evangelization and church growth in Africa is a vital movement for the salvation of lives on the continent. What it needs is visionary leadership and Spirit-filled believers. In order for The United Methodist Church to sustain the fruit of the evangelization movement in Africa, it must focus on numerical, spiritual, and financial growth. The fruit of the good news of Jesus Christ must begin with personal transformation in response to

Jesus Christ as Lord of one's life. When the lives of individual Christians are transformed by the power of the Holy Spirit, even death threats do not stop them from advancing the kingdom of God on earth.

John Russell is a retired United Methodist pastor. He has held leading positions including district superintendent and head of the Department of Evangelism in the Liberia Annual Conference.

3

Evangelization in Urban and Rural Areas

Introduction

Evangelization is a challenge that the church in the 21st century should address more than ever so the reign of the Lord will come upon the whole inhabited earth. It is faced with new realities regarding evangelization such as: the agglomeration of cities compounded by a rural exodus, and the spread of Islam.

The objective of this paper is to respond to this imperative task that The United Methodist Church in Africa, supported by the General Board of Global Ministries of The United Methodist Church, has committed to producing a resource document on evangelization and church growth. In doing so, it gives us the opportunity to reflect on evangelization in urban and rural areas. In order to achieve the goal of training both the clergy and the laity, The United Methodist Church gives us the opportunity to participate in the edification of the body of Christ in general and that of the United Methodist people in particular. This article sets out provide an objective reflection while offering a modest contribution to the development of resource. To this end, the article will address the following concerns:

1. Is it important for United Methodists in Africa to receive training on evangelization in urban and rural areas given what they are already doing?
2. What are the challenges and opportunities for evangelization in urban and rural areas? And what approach could be considered for effective evangelization?
3. What interest does this subject arouse for the African Christian?In case one doesn't show interest on this matter, what could be done cultivate it and maintain it?

To address these concerns, the article will first examine the biblical and theological background of evangelization in urban and rural areas. Then it will share about the experience of the church in Africa on evangelization, building on examples of Christian communities throughout the African continent. Then, it will present some materials on preparing for evangelization in these two environments.

Biblical Foundation of Evangelization in Urban and Rural Environments

The word "evangelism" comes from the Greek word εὐαγγελίσασθαι (euaggelizasthai). It comes from the verb εὐαγγελίζω (euaggelizo), which in the Old Testament (Septuagint) means: proclaiming the joyful news.

Old Testament

The Old Testament mentions about 119 cities. Its stories open a window on some of the major cities such as Sodom and Gomorrah, Jericho, Jerusalem, and Nineveh. Out of God's unfailing love for humankind, God sent to those big cities God's servants to spread the word, but most of them refused to listen and change.

New Testament

Jesus was born in a village and lived in a village. He visited both cities and villages during his earthly ministry.

Given the crucial task of the mission, Watson wrote "that is ultimately the task of the evangelist and herald, and to this end, he must be not only faithful to the message entrusted to him; but also dependent on the Holy Spirit who alone can glorify Christ and bring the hearers in touch with the living God."[1]

Theological Basis of Evangelization in Urban and Rural Environments in the Bible

Although some theologians look down on evangelization, and some evangelists choose to avoid theology, they are complementary for implementing the plan of salvation for humanity. One cannot do without one another. I will draw upon the doctrine of John Wesley to apply to evangelization in urban and rural areas.

This doctrine is based on divine revelation and the personal experience of John Wesley and is summarized in four declarations:[2]

1. All need to be saved (sin). This declaration speaks of sin as John Wesley described it, "the hideous leprosy of sin, that man brings from his mother's womb, covering his entire soul, and that corrupts all his capacities."[3]
2. All can be saved (repentance, justification). Based on Romans 8:1, John Wesley declared that "God doesn't condemn one who is justified and forgiven. He doesn't condemn him down here, or in the ages to come. His sins, all his past sins, sins of thought, speech or action are deleted, they won't be charged on him."[4]
3. All can know they are saved (assurance of salvation). After he returned from America and later after his conversion on the famous

night of Aldersgate, Wesley wrote in his diary, "I felt a warming in my heart, I did trust in Christ, Christ alone, for my salvation and an assurance was given me that He had taken away my sins, even mine."[5]

4. All can be saved at the highest level (sanctification). Sanctification implies learning to sin no more, coming from on Leviticus 19:2: "You shall be holy, for I the Lord your God am holy." For Wesley, this holiness meant perfect love for God and one's neighbors.[6]

The theology applicable to evangelization in urban and rural environments is from the approach of God's messengers to Jerusalem and Nineveh, and that of Jesus to Nazareth and the villages he passed through during his earthly ministry. Jon Tal Murphree believes that evangelization is, "the application of God's grace through love, expressed on the cross of Calvary to the deepest human need."[7] As it were, evangelization in cities and villages is the application of God's grace, grace through which God expresses God's love.

The Lord Jesus in his keynote speech in Luke 4:18-19 unpacks the implications of human deep need for the gospel and Matthew 28:18-20 is a command to evangelize everywhere. This need is the expressed or unexpressed desire for people to be united with their Creator and engage in a true and genuine relationship with God.

Opportunities For Evangelization In Cities And Villages

In Africa, the church is facing multiple challenges in cities and villages. These challenges can be opportunities for evangelization. Among the challenges are the advance of Islam and the actions of Islamic extremists; homelessness; poverty; globalization; prohibition on proselytization in the northern countries; multiplication of cities and the rapid growth of their populations; rebellions and civil wars; and political situations after wars and crises. This is in addition to the traditional religions, lack of spiritual maturity among many Christians, and religious syncretism. There are also stigmatized people, the disabled, those least reached or unreached, etc. All these challenges represent opportunities for the proclamation of the gospel.

Experiences of African Churches in Regards to Evangelization in Cities and Rural Areas

Joseph, a young Egyptian man created a Christian community in his neighborhood, which happens to be in a garbage dump. The Southern Baptist Church in Cairo, Egypt, trains Joseph and other pastors on the different techniques of evangelization.

In South Africa, the White River Methodist Church's committee on evangelism and mission serves in Mozambique. It supports the Wesleyan Methodist Church of Maputo for evangelization in schools and cities and opened a mission at Chikualakuala village.[8]

Through its outreach program, the Methodist Church in Kenya has provided a 10-day clinic in the coastal region providing free medical care and consultation. This activity conducted in partnership with Kenyan medical missions and doctors from the United States served the most remote villages in this region.[9]

The United Methodist Church in Côte d'Ivoire initiates evangelization ministries through the various structures of the department of Revival, Evangelism, and Mission which are: The Methodist Revival Movement (MRM), Cell for Classical Evangelism (CEC), and the Society of Methodist Missions (SMM).[10]

This work is done in collaboration with interdenominational agencies of evangelization. To date, the MRM has mobilized 200 intercessors. The CEC evangelized more than 130 cities and villages of the country, sharing the gospel with more than 15,466 people. Among them, 3,762 were led to the Lord and nurtured to be mature disciples.[11]

Cry Cameroon Ministries is concerned with preaching the gospel in Cameroon. To achieve its objectives, it has structures within itself such as a Youth Union for Mission, Women's[12] Union for Mission, Men's Union for Mission, and the Ministerial Fellowship of Pastors, which trains and sends pastors in mission.

Despite all these actions and activities, it is still important for the United Methodist people in Africa to receive training on evangelization in urban and rural environments to increase efficiency.

Evangelization Materials of Some Interdenominational Organizations

Campus Crusade for Christ, an interdenominational evangelistic organization, has a useful brochure, titled "The Four Spiritual Laws," which is very useful for evangelism at an individual level. It is available online at www.campuscrusade.com.

The material from Gideon's International is also usable for evangelism. Particularly helpful is the information on the last two pages of the small blue New Testament. Visit www.gideons.org for more information on these materials.

The manual for preparation of evangelism of the CEC from The United Methodist Church in Côte d'Ivoire is also useful. The following material is taken from that manual. In different ways, it instructs individuals and local churches how to put into practice the Great Commission.[13]

For Local Church Involvement with Evangelization

How can a local church offer an evangelistic vision to its members?

- By obeying to the commandments of Christ;
- By being a vibrant and dynamic church;
- By growing in numbers and spiritual depth.

For practical implementation, the local church may proceed as follows:

1. The pastor and elders/deacons should be models in the area of evangelization. Teachings relating to evangelization must be shared regularly from the pulpit and in Sunday school. For example, the pastor could give a series of messages as devotions from the book of Acts to teach biblical principles relating to evangelization
2. All members should be urged and encouraged to undertake training and be personally engaged in evangelization so that it becomes a way of life. They should regularly be offered an opportunity to share their testimonies to Christians and non-Christians. The testimonies of those who recently shared their faith should be regularly mentioned in meetings
3. Evangelization should be practiced outside of the church except for instances where one brings a friend, an acquaintance or a relative who is not a Christian.
4. Church members should be encouraged to write down the names of their parents, friends, and colleagues and start praying regularly for their salvation and ask God to give them an opportunity to share the gospel with them.

Before concretely starting these evangelistic activities, the church should commit them to God through prayer.

How can the church organize an evangelistic crusade?

- Gain permission from the authorities.
- Ensure that different teams are set up and at work to cover the different aspects of the crusade.

- Ensure that the advertising of the crusade is clear and reaches the targeted audience.
- Search for a location that is neutral, served by public transportation, and accessible by all for the event.
- Determine the duration and budget of the crusade.
- Ensure that the speakers have prepared their sermons, are honest, and have a heart for non-Christians.
- Organize prayer groups in the church to pray for the program and a prayer committee to work on site.
- Train effective leaders for the sessions.
- Put a worship team in place and ask them to sing as needed.
- Verify work materials and be assured of their appropriate use.
- Insist on discipline and respect guidelines during the campaign to avoid misunderstandings and disputes.
- Launch an altar call to come to Christ and allow the power of the Holy Spirit to manifest during deliverances and healings (Acts 8:6-8).
- Arrange chairs in a strategic way to facilitate orderly movement in the assembly.
- Ensure that there are enough people for supporting and coaching the new converts.
- Start the evangelistic crusade through a door-to-door evangelization campaign followed by an invitation to the meeting venue.
- Ensure that there are enough brochures for distribution and registration sheets for a good follow-up.
- Ensure that the new converts are oriented to a local church.
- Ensure that all team members share the love of God and no acts of condemnation, criticism, or inadequacy are felt by the new converts.
- Remember that in all forms of public evangelization the objective isn't to attract large numbers but to stimulate authentic disciples of Christ.

- Be dynamic, enthusiastic, entertaining, lively, and energetic.
- Put in place a committee for deliverance for the session.
- Allow the Holy Spirit to guide you in everything and act in faith by trusting in God.
- Develop a good strategy for mentoring new converts at the end of the crusade.

Different Spheres of Evangelization

The different spheres of evangelization include public and personal contact (door-to-door); non-Christian religions including Muslims; children and street children; drug dealers and addicts; pimps and prostitutes; people in hospitals, and prisons, schools and families; villages and new church plants.

Tools of Evangelization

Some tools of evangelization include music, drama, sport, and the construction of places of worship.

Some Practical Exercises for Evangelization

The following exercises can be practiced by individuals, church groups, or the whole church.

First Exercise

- Prepare oneself in prayer for 30 minutes.
- Select an unconverted person to evangelize to in one's own surrounding.

- Pray for him or her.
- Choose an appropriate circumstance and develop a friendship with the unconverted person to share the gospel with him or her.
- Read the Gospel of John for yourself.

Second Exercise

- Pray that all elements that may lead us to disobey the Lord would be banned from our lives.
- Study these texts that speak of the necessity to evangelize John 4, 1 Corinthians 9, Acts 8, and Matthew 10.
- Visit a non-Christian and start evangelizing through friendship building.

Third Exercise

- Read the Gospel of Mark.
- Know the four spiritual laws and their application.
- Adapt them to the following Bible stories:
  - Luke 8:43-48
  - Mark 5:1-20

Fourth Exercise

Approach a non-Christian and share the four spiritual laws with him or her.

- Pray the prayer of conversion if the person is ready to accept Christ and offer him or her useful advice, such as go to church, buy a Bible and read it daily, and learn to speak to God in prayer.

- Read the gospel of Matthew.

Note: This is an example of a prayer of conversion likely to be used during evangelization:

Lord Jesus I need you, I recognize that I am a sinner and that I am lost without you. I open unto you today the door of my heart and receive you as my Savior and my God. Thank you for dying on the cross for me and for the forgiveness of my sins. Give me today your new life and forever lead my life, make me the person you want me to be. Amen.

Fifth Exercise

- Share in writing the details of your conversion.
- Study the presentation of an individual testimony. Read and study the apostle Paul's two testimonies of conversion in Acts 22:1-21 and Acts 26:1-29.
- Share your testimony in front of people for 10 minutes.

Note: The content of a personal testimony includes the following:

- Who I was before Christ (my sinful life).
- How I met Christ (circumstances of my conversion).
- My life with Christ now (how I live my Christian life).

Sixth Exercise

Because the rich also need the gospel, try this approach:

- Study the story of Zacchaeus (Luke 19:1-10), the young rich man (Mark 10:17-31), the rich man and Lazarus (Luke 16:19-31), and Cornelius the Roman centurion (Acts 10)

- Write messages of evangelization from these four stories and preach them in front of an audience.
- Evangelize to a rich person in the neighborhood or a rich family member.

Seventh Exercise

Practice intercession for an evangelistic crusade.

- Pray for the following elements:
  - Location of the crusade
  - Resources
  - Souls to be won
  - The message and the messenger
  - The manifestation of the power of the Holy Spirit
- Find a location that will host an evangelistic crusade and pray for it.
- Organize fasting and prayer sessions to prepare for the evangelistic crusade.

Eighth Exercise

- Set up the following evangelization teams:
  1. Evangelists
  2. Leaders
  3. Intercessors
  4. Mentors for new converts
  5. Singers
  6. Organizers
  7. Finance people
- Develop a budget for the crusade.

- Learn songs of evangelization.
- Learn the evangelism techniques (door to door).
- Develop an information sheet for the evangelized people.

Conclusion

Evangelization has to be a necessity for the church in Africa in the 21st century so it can be more dynamic and so that the reign of the Lord Jesus Christ will come. Africa and Asia have the fastest growth and the populations of these two continents will triple in the next 40 years.[14]

Because more than 400 cities have populations exceeding one million and 21 have more than 10 million, evangelization in its various approaches must be built on a solid training education.[15]

There is a danger for a church busy with business other than God's business (mission and evangelization). A church that is not winning souls for the kingdom of God is in fact working for the kingdom of Satan. The advance of Islam and Islamic extremists' actions, homelessness, poverty, multiplication of cities and the rapid growth of their populations, rebellions and civil wars, political crises, traditional religions, lack of spiritual maturity, religious syncretism, and so forth underscore the need for Christ.

Therefore, it is important for the United Methodist Church in Africa to be trained on evangelization in urban and rural areas even if they are already involved in this work. If it happens that some local United Methodist churches do not show any interest on the matter of mission or evangelization, they need to be trained and helped to be able to transform challenges into opportunities for effective evangelization.

Rev. Pierrette Ayite Beugré is an ordained minister of The United Methodist Church, Côte d'Ivoire. She is director of Bible translation and has expertise in English and Hebrew translations of the Bible.

4

Youth and Young Adults and Their Role in Evangelization and Church

Introduction

In every generation, older people are inclined to look down on younger people. Some view young people as unimportant and unable to contribute to the development of society. As a result, they are not allowed to attend meetings with elders. In these instances, young people are expected to follow decisions made by their elders. Some governments do not involve youth in serious leadership roles, because they assume that young people lack experience. They assume youth do not have the experience to handle serious issues in government. Most of the families in Africa are organized so that the elderly make all of the decisions in the family. In some instances church leaders have contributed to this attitude towards young people. Youth, however, can play a great role in evangelization and church growth. This has been witnessed in churches where young people have been given a chance to participate in different church programs.

The purpose of this article is to lift up young people as a resource and suggest roles they can play in evangelization and church growth in Africa. The Old and New Testaments are filled with examples of young people who made a difference that can be related to today's context. This article also explores the role that patriarchy, which is common throughout Africa, plays in the lives of young men and women. Young people contribute to the growth and development of the church and this article will highlight some areas in which youth are participating. It also highlights the challenges young people in East Africa face and how the church can help them overcome these barriers to live out their true potential.

Definition of Terms

Youth and Young Adults

The Book of Discipline of the United Methodist Church, 2012, ¶1210 defines youth as those from 12 to 18 years old and young adults as those from 19 to 30 years old.[1]

The Uganda National Youth Policy defines youth as all persons, female and male, aged 12 to 30 years. This is a period of great emotional, physical, and psychological change that requires societal support for a safe passage from adolescence to full adulthood. The United Nations describes youth as persons from the ages 14 to 24, while the African youth charter defines a youth as a person between the ages of 15 and 35 years old.[2,3]

Therefore, this article concerns youth and young adults from 12 to 35 years old.

Evangelization

Dr. John Wesley Kurewa defines evangelization as something broader in scope or more comprehensive than the term evangelism. Evangelization embraces all the ministries or activities of the church. He further says that right from the beginning, missionary evangelization of Africa included evangelism, education, health care, agriculture, and many other activities.[4]

Church Growth

George G. Hunter, distinguished professor and emeritus of Asbury Theological Seminary's School of World Mission and Evangelism, defines church growth as a clue or indicator of a church's profitable vitality, seriousness, and effectiveness.[5]

Patriarchal Society in Africa

In Africa, patriarchy is real and it can hamper young women and men in the church and community. This has had impact on the lives of both young men and women as servants of God.

Patriarchy is the term used to describe the society in which we live today, which is characterized by the current and historic unequal power relations between women and men, whereby women are systematically disadvantaged and oppressed. This takes place across almost every sphere of life, but is particularly noticeable in women's underrepresentation in key state institutions, decision-making positions, and employment and industry. Male violence against women is also a key feature of patriarchy. Women in minority groups face multiple oppressions in this society, as race, class, and sexuality intersect with sexism.[6]

How Patriarchy Plays Out in the Life of the Church

In most churches and ministries, women and youth are viewed as valuable workers, as they often do the majority of the overall ministry. Yet not all churches agree on what roles women and youth should have. Women and youth are often restricted from certain areas of ministry within the church that pertain to speaking and leadership. Some churches accept female pastors and teachers, yet many others do not. Some restrict women from speaking at all during church services. Most of these disagreements hinge on various interpretations of Paul's words regarding women's roles in 1 Corinthians 14:34-35, 1 Timothy 2:11-12, and 1 Corinthians 11:3.

Debra Simpson notes in a Mennonite Central Committee paper that patriarchy originates from both culture and the Bible and settles properly in church. People who go to church come from cultural backgrounds and they carry it all to the church.[7]

My personal view is that patriarchy affects not only women but also young people in general. Their level of participation in decision-making and leadership is still wanting; they are underrepresented in church leadership positions. Many people in the older generations believe that if youth are given serious responsibilities, they will mess up things, so it is best to limit their participation.

Similarly, in communities when a young man or woman rises up for a leadership position, political or otherwise, the person is considered too young for the position if male, and intimidated if female.

The church has selectively used the Bible to promote the submissiveness of women and the dominance of men. Instead of being a prophetic voice in this world, the church is seen to be behind patriarchy in most parts of Africa.

Likewise, girls in many communities are forced into marriage at a young age because their culture dictates that they must have a man to look after them. They have been made to believe that they have to depend on men. Early marriage is especially common for those who have not had the chance to pursue an education.

Also due to patriarchy, a girl child's father often pays little attention to her education. Some men still believe it is useless to pay girls' school fees, because they could be married off at any time. As a result, women are unable to compete favorably with men in socioeconomic and political issues. In addition, girls are the ones who stay at home to do housework with their mothers, while boys do little at home and enjoy playing outside or join their fathers for conversation.

The Bible clearly says that: "There is no longer Jew nor Greek, there is no longer slave or free, there is no longer male and female; for all of you are one in Christ Jesus" (Galatians 3:28, NRSV).

The Bible also records God's declaration: "I will pour out my Spirit upon all flesh, and your sons and your daughters shall prophesy, and your young men shall see visions, and your old men shall dream dreams" (Acts 2:17, NRSV).

Young People in the Bible

The Bible as a whole informs us about how God involves young people, both male and female, in redemptive, prophetic, and pastoral ministries. The following are some examples in both testaments of the Bible. The scripture passages provide a starting place to learn about the biblical figures.

- Joseph (Genesis 37-50)
- Samuel (1 Samuel 3)
- David (1 Samuel 16-17; 2 Samuel 6; Psalm 51)
- Jeremiah (Jeremiah 1)
- Ruth (Ruth 1-4)
- Timothy (1 Timothy 1)
- Titus (Titus 1)
- Mary, the mother of Jesus (Luke 1:26-55)

Challenges Young People Face Today

The National Youth Policy of Uganda (2001) indicates that the lives of many Ugandan youth are marred by multiple challenges. "The environment they live in brings both new possibilities and new risks that undermine the traditional social support that helps the youth prepare for, negotiate, and explore the opportunities and demands of their passage to adulthood."[8]

In Uganda alone, youth ages 15-19 constitute 29 percent of the country's population.[9]

A trend of rural-urban migration by youth is observable. They are moving to urban centers to search for better social services and amenities like education and health services; to search for employment and business opportunities; and also to escape insecurity, domestic violence, and parental neglect.[10]

Some of the many challenges that affect young people include the following:

Poverty: This is a serious social problem among the young people in Africa. It is due to lack of resources for the high population of youth in Africa. Most young people in the rural areas cannot access quality education and therefore have to engage in subsistence farming, which does not enable them to come out of poverty. Unemployment and a high cost of living are additional causes of poverty among the young people.

Lack of access to resources, including land and capital: Young people will remain redundant if they have no resources, which they can use to empower themselves. These resources are in the hands of elders and some others.

Peer pressure: Friends and others of the same generation that provide a bad influence for young people.

Lack of good role models/mentors: Adults seem to spend less time with young people due to recent socioeconomic changes. People are too busy and give little attention to guiding children and youth. Many young people who lack role models and mentors can cause trouble in their communities and churches, such as not wanting to work and gambling.

Mentors are necessary to counsel and guide young people. They can help shape the lives and characters of young people.

Diseases: Diseases such as HIV and AIDS, malaria, and tuberculosis are threats to young people today in Africa.

Exploitation: Many youth are exploited as a source for cheap labor, but the wages do not meet their financial needs. Consequently, they resort to stealing to fill the gaps and as a result, they are arrested and end up in prison.

Civil unrest and displacement: Many young people have lost their lives as a result of war.

Gender discrimination: Primarily women experience gender discrimination. They are usually not considered important and as a result, their contributions to society are constrained.

Inadequate work/employment opportunities: Many youth are unemployed in the East Africa Annual Conference: 62 percent of the youth in Uganda are unemployed, 65 to 80 percent of youth in Kenya are unemployed, and 28.9 percent of youth in Rwanda were unemployed in 2005,[11,12,13]

Other East African countries such as Burundi and South Sudan have similar numbers of unemployed youth.

This level of unemployment poses a serious security challenge in the East African region where wars, violence, terrorism, drug abuse, and tribal conflicts are frequent.

Unwanted pregnancy: Many young women get pregnant when they are not ready for it and have abortions.

Manipulation of youth by politicians: Youth are often used to fight battles for politicians. They are involved in risky demonstrations and arguments. They are convinced to join rebel groups while others are kidnapped. This has been witnessed in the northern part of Uganda where youth have been fighting a purposeless war for over two decades. Most of them lost their lives during this war.

Effects of these Challenges on Communities and Churches

Due to poverty and unemployment, many youth are involved in activities such as drinking, gambling, and drug abuse. As a result, they often turn against society as rapists, robbers, and petty thieves. Young girls engage in commercial sex and are married young, whereby they end up infected with sexually transmitted diseases and may not be able to care for themselves without the help of their community or church.

Young women suffer much as a result of getting pregnant early in life, because they are the most vulnerable. They are the ones who care for the children and will give up any development programs in order to look after the baby. The church and their parents need to help these young women.

When young people become sick, imprisoned, and or even die because they have made poor choices, society loses their contributions. The church can be overwhelmed by work to care for and nurture vulnerable young people.

Youth can contribute a lot to evangelization and church growth in Africa, but the effects of poverty, unemployment, and diseases such as HIV/AIDS force them to give a low priority to God's work.

Educational Opportunities for Youth

Vocational education and skills are important to empower youth. Young people in East Africa have a lot of educational opportunities, which include the following:

- Vocational training programs in Uganda increase the skills of young people. This is believed to be the best way to eradicate unemployment and poverty and enable youth to become job creators and not job seekers.

- Universal primary education is offered in Kenya and Uganda, allowing children to access free education and training. Uganda's free education system goes up to high school.
- Universities are accessible to youth from families who have an average income. For example, a number of youth have attended Africa University and have returned with skills that allow them to be contributing members of society.

The Church's Response to the Challenges of Young People

Young people need leaders who will be empathetic to young people, understand the issues that are unique to them, and involve them in programs that are relevant to them. Leaders need to bring young people closer to them, look into their challenges, and offer help. The church should know how to respond to the expectations of young people, and allow them to participate in mission and church work. Young people in general have a hunger for connection, relationship, and belonging.

Church leaders need to develop youth group activities that generate interest in the local community, reinforce devotional habits, and create lasting connections between the young people in a congregation and their community. Planning activities that create a strong youth group will help the young people to lead a good Christian life by building a strong support group of faith in the church.

Christian youth ministries serve a crucial role in moving Christian churches forward. Youth ministry leaders should challenge young people to find and keep Christ at the center of their daily lives. As they mature, they will become leaders in their churches and serve as role models for the rest of the members. Spiritual discipline usually does not come naturally, but grows over time as young people face challenges. Youth ministers teach Christian values through any number of activities designed to guide Christian young people toward fulfilling lives of service to God.

Discipleship should be a priority for churches so that young people will develop a strong faith and love for God.

The church should seek to understand the needs and challenges that young people face and offer to address them. Young people need someone who will show them direction and hope for tomorrow.

Income-generating projects such as farming for rural youth, brick making, and offering technical and vocational skills training needs to be established. Some churches such as Anglican and Catholic churches have technical schools at their mission centers to address the problem of unemployment and poverty, which other church organizations should emulate.

There are many other activities that the church could develop to support young people, such as the following suggestions.

Music programs can motivate young people. They need to be involved in choir, praise, worship, and music festivals.

Drama is very important for youth and should address the needs of young people. The content should be based on the Bible and real-life situations.

Youth outings in the form of seminars, conferences, and retreats are very important as they help youth learn through discussions, and therefore the church should organize these. The church can also empower young people as they discuss in detail how God loves them. It also gives them time to reflect on God's presence in their lives. They can share testimonies and different experiences at these outings, so that each of them is given a chance to speak about a number of issues.

Youth camps can act as centers for restoration and rehabilitation with the right programs and activities. Through these camps, the presence of love, hope, and God's peace can transform lives. They can also help rebuild broken lives. Youth can get away from their worries and discover relationships.

Youth days in churches are very important, whereby young people have the opportunity to lead a worship service through music, preaching, and other aspects of the worship service.

Youth funds allow young people to borrow money at low interest rates to start up some businesses. This would help meet the needs of youth in the church that are out of school and unemployed. Through the funds, they could create jobs for themselves and for others.

Other programs that can be created to empower and excite the youth could include the following:

- Guidance and counseling to help young people achieve objectives that impact their careers and personal, social, educational, economic life.
- Games and sports to not only help keep young people healthy but also for team building, exposure to new experiences, and promotion of interactions through which young people can develop new ways of solving issues in their lives.
- Scouting programs to contribute to the development of young people in achieving their full physical, intellectual, social, and spiritual potentials to prepare them to be responsible adults.

Why Young People are Instrumental in Evangelization and Church Growth

The following are some reasons young people are needed in the church's evangelization and church growth efforts:

- Young people have more free time to participate in church activities, which contributes to evangelization and church growth in the areas of music, revivals, evangelism, youth conferences, and festivals, among others.

- Young people generally are strong and energetic. They can participate fully in church programs without becoming easily tired.
- Young people are very ambitious. They typically want to achieve something and also want to please their leaders and, if given time, they can contribute a lot to the growth of the church.
- Professional young people can contribute to professional ministries. For instance, some young people are teachers, doctors, engineers, and social workers.

Story of Mr. Kunya Ronald

Mr. Kunya Ronald is 27 years old and is from Jinja, Uganda. He is an agriculturalist and department head for agriculture in a Ugandan institution. Mr. Kunya comes from a humble background. He was raised by a single father because his mother passed on when he was very young. Life was very hard because Mr. Kunya's father was just a rural peasant. He says that he had, however, managed to study up to high school.

He shared with me that when he was in grade four in secondary school, he had friends who were hooligans and stubborn. They tried to lure him into their activities and when he joined them for a while, he realized this life was not good for him. When he realized that he was losing some values by spending time with them, he decided to distance himself from them completely and this helped him to concentrate at high school and excel in his academics.

Mr. Kunya joined a national teachers college on government sponsorship and graduated with a diploma in education, majoring in agriculture. He got a job and after working for some time, he enrolled for a bachelor's degree in agriculture. Currently, he is pursuing his master's degree.

Mr. Kunya attributed his achievement to his relationship with Jesus. He became a Christian during his senior six vacation. God has been faithful to this young man. The boys who wanted to lead him astray are now dead. Mr Kunya said that, had he not distanced himself from them, he could have died too.

He is now a great evangelist and servant of God. He has a revival amongst his friends. His brothers and sister who had dropped out of school have begun acquiring job skills through his ministry. He is helping many young people to see their direction. God has done a lot through him beyond what man could do alone.

The impact of his life on many youth and his family makes him stronger in the Lord every day. He says that what he is today is just the beginning. God is about to do great things in his life.

Mr. Kunya gives the following advice to young people:

- Time and age are important but should not prevent one from trusting God and having a vision in life.
- The future is always bright; one only needs to be focused.
- Today's struggles are not final. Tomorrow will be different.

Story of Ms. Rose Martha

Ms. Rose Martha, age 34, was born in a polygamous family. However, her father divorced her mother because she had given birth to only girl children. Although her father was a teacher, their community viewed girls as a source of income. They could be married off any time and get money from the men and therefore they were not worthy of being accorded formal education. Life was never the same for Ms. Rose after her mother's divorce.

At age 12, Ms. Rose accepted Jesus Christ as her Lord and Savior and chose to trust God to re-align her future knowing well that the world did not have much to offer her. As the first born in her family, Ms. Rose knew she had to be a role model. Although she was very engaged in different ministries in the church including evangelism, choir, Bible studies, and youth ministry, Ms. Rose would work to supplement what the mother could afford to offer for her school fees. She thus tried to strike a balance between church ministry, family, and school. Consequently, she was entrusted with various leadership positions in the church.

Ms. Rose used her leadership positions not only to influence her siblings but also to influence many of her friends to accept Jesus Christ as Lord and Savior. Just as any young girl growing up, Ms. Rose faced a number of challenges resulting from limited resources, adolescence, and choice of career. She is now a professional engineer and instructor who has risen through the ranks. She is not only a blessing as a civil servant in Uganda but also to her church. She has been able to influence many youth to become self-reliant, and desist from prostitution and drug-abuse by encouraging them to attain vocational education and training.

Ms. Rose is now married and serving as the president for United Methodist Women in Uganda. She became president at age 28. Following is some advice from Ms. Rose:

- God loves all people regardless of gender. I chose to pursue an engineering course to prove to my people that male or female, we have all been blessed with knowledge, wisdom, and abilities that we can exploit for God's glory.
- No matter the circumstances that you go through in life, provided you do not lose focus, the future will always be bright. If you trust your future with God, you will never be disappointed.
- God is the master programmer of our lives and as such he will always use our testimonies to edify others.

- I chose to contest for the presidency of United Methodist Women in order to speak for the "unheard" and inspire other marginalized youth.

Ms. Rose is resilient, focused, and hardworking. She believes God blesses her work so that she can bless others.

Conclusion

Youth often find themselves the middle of things. They are neither children nor adults. They undergo a lot of maturation during these years including physical, social, spiritual, and intellectual growth. They need a lot of help to balance life as they develop. The Bible is full of stories about youth who were engaged in great ministries and exhibited great faith. God called both young women and men to complete specific assignments. God is doing the same for young people today. Let young people learn from Timothy and Titus, who led churches at a young age and instructed elderly people in the ways of God. Youth should be exemplary in speech, in faith, in love, in spirit, and in purity to earn respect from elders and become very instrumental in evangelization and church growth.

The Rev. Musooko Moses is the district superintendent, Kamuli District, Uganda, East Africa Annual Conference. He is a teacher at the United Methodist Bible College and an instructor (electrical) at Kakira Technical Institute. He is involved in church planting and development work in his district.

5

How to Develop A Bible Study

Introduction

Bible study helps us to put into practice what the Word of God says (1 Corinthians 10:11; 2 Thessalonians 3:4). Knowledge of God's Word empowers Christ's followers. This article seeks to provide guidelines on how one can go about developing a Bible study. Its goal is to provide information and guidance for persons leading Bible studies at academies for evangelization and church growth. This guide can also be used in other settings where Bible studies are done.

This Bible study guide has been written so that it meets the demands of an African Christian believer. It has been designed in such a way that it can be used in different settings such as in families, home groups, specific small groups (e.g., support groups, section meetings), Sunday school, or by individuals who intend to engage in personal Bible study. The text selected for this guide is Matthew 28:16-20, the Great Commission. The article stipulates the benefit of Bible study, ways in which we are to assimilate the Bible, and the steps to consider when developing a Bible study.

What is the Benefit of Studying the Bible?

The Bible is the plenary, verbal, inspired, and infallible Word of the only true and living God. It is the Holy Book. It is a special book, written by different authors, inspired by the Holy Spirit. In the Bible we find answers to life's[1,2,3,4] greatest questions: Where did I come from? What is my purpose? Where am I going with my life? Despite the fact that the Bible is made up of various books, it has one central theme: God's plan for saving humanity.

Through Bible study we come to understand what God is like, that is, God's thoughts, plans, and promises; know that God is Holy, and God is near to those who call on his name in truth (Psalm 145:18); know that God is all knowing (Hebrews 4:13); and know that God is all powerful (1 Chronicles 29:11). We also realize that God's Word is a light to our lives (2 Peter 1:19), it gives understanding in a dark world. God's Word abides forever. It does not fade. It is God's letter to us (John 3:16; Romans 5:8). It is God's sword of the Spirit (Ephesians 6:17; Hebrews 4:12). It is the source of our faith (Romans 10:8). The Bible is the rule or standard by which we determine what is right and what is wrong. It is full of true unreachable riches (Ephesians 3:8). It is filled with many wonderful, life-sustaining promises (Isaiah 41:10; Exodus 33:14; Philippians 4:6-7). God's Word gives guidance (Psalms 119:165) and meaning to life. The Word of God has wonderful transforming power. It has delivered many from the bondage of sin. It has helped many to live noble, beautiful lives. It has enabled people to live well with their families, children, friends, neighbors, and communities. It enables young people to stay pure (Psalm 119:9-10). How amazing is the Word of God? Bible study time helps us to grow in the Lord and our capacity to understand God's Word and will.

Ways That We Are to Assimilate the Word of God in our Lives

Homer Duncan, founder of the Missionary Crusader, suggested five methods to consider when studying the Bible. In my faith journey I have applied these methods of Bible study and found them appropriate. We are to assimilate (take in) the Bible in the following ways:[5]

1. **By hearing it:** Paul posed these questions in Romans 10:14: "But how are they to call on one in whom they have not believed? And how are they to believe in one of whom they have never heard? And how are they to hear without someone to proclaim him?" (NRSV) During Bible study sessions, we should not rush, we have to read and listen attentively to the message we hear through preachers, teachers of the Bible, music, and anything that teaches about God's Word.
2. **By reading it:** When you read the Bible, your mind must be on what you are reading. The Bible speaks primarily to the heart. We must read God's Word with honest hearts and open minds. The Bible is Christ in print. As we read it earnestly we will meet the Lord Jesus Christ, our wonderful Savior and Redeemer and he will convict us of our sins. The Holy Spirit will cleanse us and transforms our lives. Establish a culture of reading God's Word each day.
3. **By studying it:** Study the Bible as a whole and then study it book-by-book, chapter-by-chapter, verse-by-verse, and then word-by-word. Studying the Bible gives us knowledge. Our goal in studying the Bible is to know the deep things of God. We must search the scriptures every day. Daily Bible study feeds our spirits; just as we need physical food, we also require spiritual food. We need to study the Bible with honest hearts and open minds to learn what the Bible says, and not what we think the Bible says. Most Christian believers fail in their faith journey because they do not study the Bible. Most preachers fail to deliver because they have no message, which is a product of intensive Bible study. The Holy Spirit inspires us when we take ample time to study God's Word.

4. **By memorizing it:** The Psalmist says, "I have hidden your word in my heart that I might not sin against you" (Psalm 119:11, NIV). Memorizing verses has helped me with studying the Bible. The first verse I memorized was John 3:16: "For God so loved the world that he gave his only Son, so that everyone who believes in him may not perish but may have eternal life." (NRSV) Start by memorizing short verses and then work towards memorizing chapters. Other passages are easier to memorize because they have been composed into hymns. Memorizing Bible verses keeps us connected to God and enables us to know God's will for our existence.
5. **By meditating upon it:** This is the most important way of assimilating the Bible into your life. We are to meditate on God's Word day and night. A person who meditates on God's Word will prosper in everything he or she does (Psalm 1:2-3; Joshua 1:8). To meditate is to ruminate, to bring to mind and consider over and over. Ruminating is what a cow does when it chews the cud. During meditation you are reflecting on what you are going to do with what you have learned. The Psalmist asked the question in Psalm 119:9,[6] "How can young people keep their way pure?" The response, "By guarding it according to your word," means that they should meditate on God's Word all the time.

After going through these methods, we should be saturated with God's Word so that it will spontaneously flow from our lives. To be a witness, we must be filled with God's Word. We cannot all be pastors, preachers, or teachers, but every Christian can be a witness for Christ (Acts 1:8).

Steps to Consider When Developing a Bible Study

There are several steps to consider when conducting a Bible study. Some of these steps include: surveying the Bible, analyzing the text, and applying what you learned. The key element to every step is prayer. Pray for inspiration and revelation. Pray for leaders and participants. The more you pray for each other, the more you will love each other with God's love.

You may begin by training leaders to lead Bible study sessions or groups. It is crucial to assess the needs of your congregation and/or group members. This will help when establishing small groups for Bible study and Sunday school. It will also guide your selection of books and texts to be studied. Your Bible study must be Christ-centered, flexible (able to deal with changing situations), and definite (clearly stated and specific). Participants must have the unquenchable conviction that Jesus is the key to life and death. Make the time in a group worthwhile. Application of God's word is crucial, as new disciples need to be strengthened. A community life of sharing, worship, and prayer should surround each new convert to help her or him grow in the faith.

Prepare the lessons thoroughly. Read widely. Ask the Holy Spirit to help you understand the texts. Provide material for each group member to use during discussions. Read and use different Bible versions during your preparation. Specify your goals and objectives for a particular Bible study. Visualize the outcome and impact of your Bible study.

Step 1: Surveying the Bible

In this section we will:

- Make an overview of the entire Bible.
- Make a summary of each book.
- Make a Bible synthesis.
- Prepare a simple outline of each book.

Make an overview of the entire Bible

Participants must know the composition of the Bible. Allow each member to name the books, 39 from Old Testament and 27 from New Testament.

The English word 'bible' is derived from the Greek word, ta bliblia, "the books," and Latin biblia, "books." "The term derives from bublos or bublion, loan words from Egypt, originally denoting the stalk and the inner pitch of the papyrus plant from which scrolls were commonly made."[7] The Bible is a composition of the primary religious texts for Judaism and Christianity. Some biblical scholars regard the Bible as a library, because it is composed of various books written by various authors.

The Old Testament can be grouped as follows: The five books of Moses, which contains the Law, the instruction, or the Torah, followed by the historic books from Joshua to Esther, the poetic books from Job to Song of Solomon and the prophetic books from Isaiah to Malachi. Bruce Metzger explains:

> The Old Testament demonstrates the call of a special people to enter into a covenant relationship with the God of justice and steadfast love and to bring God's law to the nations. The New Testament records the life and work of Jesus Christ, the one in whom "the Word became flesh," as well as describes the rise and spread of the early Christian Church. The Bible carries the message to all persons and communities who read it so that they may discern and understand what God is saying to them.[8]

The New Testament is a collection of 27 books that can be grouped as follows:

The Gospels: Matthew, Mark, Luke, and John; the Acts of the Apostles or the Acts of the Holy Spirit; the Pauline Epistles: Romans, 1 and 2 Corinthians, Galatians, Ephesians, Philippians, Colossians, 1 and 2 Thessalonians; Pastoral Letters: 1 and 2 Timothy, Titus, Philemon, and Hebrews; General Epistles, also called Jewish Epistles: James, 1 and 2 Peter, 1, 2, and 3 John, and Jude; and finally, Revelation or the Apocalypse.

Make a summary of each book

Make a Bible Synthesis method

This is the method of seeing the Bible as a whole. Dr. James M. Gray proposed six rules to this effect.[9]

- Begin with Genesis—the beginnings.
- Read the book; do not study it in the usual sense.
- Read the book continuously, at a single sitting without noticing chapters or verses.
- Read it repeatedly.
- Read it independently without commentaries.
- Read it prayerfully, depending on the Holy Spirit.

Let the reading be pleasure to you. Do not try to understand everything you read. As you continue to read you will gain understanding. Bible Synthesis is preparatory for the other methods of Bible study. To use this method, I prepared a daily Bible reading for my family, which I referred to as "A quadrennium with the Bible." For four years we read the Bible from Genesis to Revelation.

Prepare an outline of each book

A simple outline of the book you are studying will give you an overall picture. Make your outline as simple as possible according to your level of understanding. I have provided the following outline of the Gospel according to Matthew as an example:

1. Jesus is born (Chapters 1-4:11).
2. John the Baptist prepares the way for Jesus (Chapter 3).
3. Jesus has power over temptations (Chapter 4:1-11).
4. Jesus gives the Sermon on the Mount (Chapters 5-7).
5. Jesus performs miracles (Chapters 8-9).

6. Jesus sends the 12 disciples on a mission (Chapter 10).
7. Jesus gives lessons on the kingdom of God (Chapters 11-25; 46).
8. Jesus fulfills his mission (death, resurrection, and Ascension) (Chapters 26-28).
9. Jesus gives the Great Commission (Chapter 28:16-20).

Step 2: Select a Book to Study

Duncan calls this method Bible analysis and he refers to it as the "microscope."[10] In this method, the details of the book you are studying are examined or analyzed. The following questions are crucial: Who is the author and who is the audience? Where was the book written? When was it written? Why was it written, or for what purpose? How is the message applicable to our present situation?

In synthesis the Bible is taken as a whole, in analysis it is taken apart and each section is examined. After the book has been arranged in outline, the next step then is to arrange each chapter of the book you are studying under separate headings. For example, The Gospel of Matthew reports six of the lessons of Jesus. The first lesson is the Sermon on the Mount, which contains the Beatitudes, the golden rule, and the Lord's Prayer. The second lesson is in Chapter 10, which tells how the gospel should be preached. The third lesson is in Chapter 13, which explains the growth of the Kingdom through a series of the parables or stories. The fourth lesson, from Chapter 18 is about forgiveness and humility. The fifth lesson, Chapter 23, is a rebuke to the Pharisees because of their hypocrisy. The sixth lesson in Chapters 24 and 25 is a prophecy of the destruction of Jerusalem and the end of the world. These lessons give a clear picture of the beautiful message Jesus gave to the people of his day.

It is important for us to understand the context in which the author wrote the book we are studying. For instance, to understand the Great

Commission in Matthew 28:16-20, we first need to understand the entire Gospel and what the author implies about the mission work. A close look into this Gospel enables us to discover that Matthew's focus was not on the life of Jesus Christ, but on giving guidance to a community in crisis about how it should understand its calling and mission. In other words there is need to first consider the nature of the community where this task is to be carried out. This is important, since the needs and challenges of our communities vary from one community to the other. This understanding enables participants to select methods and content that is relevant to address the needs of a particular community. In Matthew's[11] community, the Pharisees were placing emphasis on the observation of the law, while the followers of Christ regarded themselves as filled with the Holy Spirit, through whom they performed miracles. Matthew's[12] task as he wrote his Gospel was to prepare the way for reconciliation, forgiveness, and mutual love within the community. He seems to suggest that the confusion, tension, and conflict that divided one group from another could only be overcome if they joined hands and hearts in a mission to the Gentiles among whom they lived.[13]

Select the Chapter, Passage, or Text

The chapter selected for this example is Matthew 28, which can be divided into four sections as follows:

1. The Resurrection of Jesus the King (verses 1-7)
2. Jesus the King's appearance to the women (verses 8-10)
3. Religious leaders bribe the guards (verses 11-15)
4. Jesus Christ's Great Commission to the apostles (verses 16-20).

Next, prayerfully study the chapter verse by verse as the Holy Spirit guides you. The Holy Spirit gives us an understanding of the scriptures.

Connect the verse you are studying with other verses in other portions of the Bible. For the sake of this article I have selected the last section of Matthew 28:16-20. My focus is on the 2013-2016 quadrennium theme, of making disciples of Jesus Christ for the transformation of the world.

How Does One Develop Questions for Different Texts?

After reading a text, ask questions to guide your Bible discussions such as: what, where, when, why, who, and how. What is the text about? What happened? Where was the scene or occasion? When did this take place? Why was this story written? Who are the persons involved in the story? How applicable is the information to your situation? The questions are directed to the text or passage. It is recommended that participants work in pairs or groups. Each participant is given room to effectively make his/her contributions. Reread the passage and underline or highlight where the answers to the questions are found in the passage. The following Bible study on Matthew 28:16-20 is a demonstration to this effect. Remember that the nature of the passage selected guides the types of questions to be asked.

Matthew 28:16-20: The Great Commission

> [16]Now the eleven disciples went to Galilee, to the mountain to which Jesus had directed them. [17]When they saw him, they worshiped him; but some doubted. [18]And Jesus came and said to them, "All authority in heaven and on earth has been given to me. [19]Go therefore and make disciples of all nations, baptizing them in the name of the Father and of the Son and of the Holy Spirit, [20]and teaching them to obey everything that I have commanded you. And remember, I am with you always, to the end of the age." (NRSV)

Every believer has a mandate to go and make disciples in the community in which he/she lives. In the Great Commission, the following questions can be raised:

1. Where did the Commissioning take place?
2. What is the nature of Jesus' command?
3. Who are the persons in the text and what are their roles? Who is the audience?
4. How are they going to carry out this task? That is, what strategies are they to embark on?
5. How far was Jesus' commission extended?
6. When were they expected to carry out this task and how long was it going to take?
7. Why should they engage themselves in this mission of making disciples of all nations?
8. What assurance did they have as they carried out this task?

Where did the Commissioning take place?

> [16]Now the eleven disciples went to Galilee, to the mountain to which Jesus had directed them. [17]When they saw him, they worshiped him; but some doubted. [18]And Jesus came and said to them, "All authority in heaven and on earth has been given to me. [19]Go therefore and make disciples of all nations, baptizing them in the name of the Father and of the Son and of the Holy Spirit, [20]and teaching them to obey everything that I have commanded you. And remember, I am with you always, to the end of the age."

This great final scene took place in Galilee on the mountain. Jesus had been betrayed, abandoned, slandered and condemned, whipped, and crucified. Galilee is in the region of northern Palestine that is situated between the Litany River in modern Lebanon and the Jezreel Valley in modern Israel. This is the area in which Jesus conducted the major part of his ministry. The mountain was part of Matthew's[14] pattern of portraying Jesus in terms of Moses, the great lawgiver of Israel (Matthew 2:15). Matthew understands that the advent of Jesus brought something new (Matthew 9:17). The location of the mountain is not geographical but theological. The mountain location recalls Moses on Sinai receiving the Decalogue. The location anticipates the revelation of God's presence. Probably, this was the same mountain in which Jesus was transfigured (Matthew 17:1).

What is the nature of Jesus' command?

> 16Now the eleven disciples went to Galilee, to the mountain
> to which Jesus had directed them. 17When they saw him, they
> worshiped him; but some doubted. 18And Jesus came and
> said to them, "All authority in heaven and on earth has been
> given to me. 19Go therefore and make disciples of all nations,
> baptizing them in the name of the Father and of the Son and
> of the Holy Spirit, 20and teaching them to obey everything
> that I have commanded you. And remember, I am with you
> always, to the end of the age."

Jesus' decree has three parts: the claim to authority, which occurred in the past (v. 18); the commission or command, which is pointing to the present (v. 19); and the motivation or promise, which is about the future (v. 20).

Who are the persons in the text and what are their roles? Who is the audience?

> 16Now the eleven disciples went to Galilee, to the mountain
> to which Jesus had directed them. 17When they saw him, they

> worshiped him; but some doubted. [18]And Jesus came and said to them, "All authority in heaven and on earth has been given to me. [19]Go therefore and make disciples of all nations, baptizing them in the name of the Father and of the Son and of the Holy Spirit, [20]and teaching them to obey everything that I have commanded you. And remember, I am with you always, to the end of the age."

It is obvious that "who" is referring to people, and they are easy to spot. You can mark references to "who" in the text. In this case we have the 11 disciples, Jesus, disciples who are to be made, all nations, the Father, the Son, and the Holy Spirit. The role each one plays in the passage should also be identified. See below for an example:

The eleven disciples: They saw and worshiped Jesus. But some among them doubted. Those who see Jesus with an eye of faith are able to worship him without doubt. Here we are not told who exactly among the eleven doubted Jesus. The eleven are the ones given the mandate to go and make disciples.

Jesus: The Messiah, the King of kings and Lord of lords, is the one giving the command. Jesus affirms that all power/authority is given to him. Jesus asserts his universal domination as Mediator, which is the great foundation of Christianity.

Disciples who are to be made: These are the ones who are enrolled as students into the school of Jesus Christ. They must be trained for Christ Jesus' service. They have to obey all that Christ has commanded with an eye to command and do as God wills, without exception, all the moral duties and all the instituted ordinances.

All nations: According to Matthew this refers to all the people, including the marginalized, for example, the poor (Matthew 5:3; 11:5; 19:21); children (Matthew 18:2-5; 19:14-15); the blind and lame (Matthew 21:14-16); the weary and those that are carrying heavy burdens (Matthew

11:28); the powerless (Matthew 18:6, 10, 14; 10:42); and the least ones of all (Matthew 25:40, 45). The nations refer to the Jews and Gentiles (Matthew 2:23; 12:18-21). The Great Commission, in this context, is a universal command, "Make disciples of all nations." All, implying that no one should be left out.

The Father and the Son and the Holy Spirit: The new disciples are to be baptized in the name of the Father, the Son, and the Holy Spirit.

How were they going to carry out this task? That is, what strategy were they to embark on?

> [16]Now the eleven disciples went to Galilee, to the mountain to which Jesus had directed them. [17]When they saw him, they worshiped him; but some doubted. [18]And Jesus came and said to them, "All authority in heaven and on earth has been given to me. [19]Go therefore and make disciples of all nations, baptizing them in the name of the Father and of the Son and of the Holy Spirit, [20]and teaching them to obey everything that I have commanded you. And remember, I am with you always, to the end of the age."

The Apostle's Task

To go: This is the great missionary commission that concerns the present. It contains the general command to go and make disciples, and has two subordinate clauses, which explain how this is to be done. How were they to go? With authority. They were to go with faith and confidence. They were motivated by the experience of knowing the living Lord and the authority of the resurrected Lord. The knowledge of the one whom they worshiped became the source of joy, peace, and power for their missionary zeal. What the disciples were going to do was not a new thing. They were to carry on Jesus' ministry. They were to teach converts won to faith and baptized to observe all that Jesus had taught. They were clear of their mission, what they were going to do, to make disciples of all nations, to baptize them and teach them the truth about God.

To make disciples: The key expression of the Great Commission, according to Matthew, is making disciples (matheteuein). The theme of discipleship is central to Matthew's Gospel and to his understanding of the church and mission. The verb matheteuin, "to make disciples," is the principal verb in the Great Commission and the heart of the commissioning. The two principles, baptizing and teaching, are clearly subordinate to matheteusate, and describe the form the disciple making should take.

To baptize: This baptism must be administered in the name of the Father and of the Son and of the Holy Spirit, i.e., by authority from heaven, and not from man for God's ministers act by authority from the Trinity who all concur as to our creation so to our redemption. By being baptized in the Godhead, we solemnly confess our belief that there is but one God in the Godhead: Father, Son, and Holy Spirit.

To teach: Teaching is the final part of the Great Commission, which highlights the most important thing to be done in the process of making disciples. Teaching them and baptizing them appear to be the real content of disciple making and, therefore, of the mission in Matthew's understanding.

Teach the way Jesus taught. Jesus had authority to teach God's truth. He showed this authority when he taught. The people who heard Jesus saw this, and they listened to him. The guards who were sent to arrest Jesus went back to their leaders alone. They said, "Never has anyone spoken like this!" (John 7:46). Jesus taught people what God's law meant to them in their everyday lives and how he had a plan for them.

How far was Jesus' Commission extended?

> 16Now the eleven disciples went to Galilee, to the mountain
> to which Jesus had directed them. 17When they saw him, they

> worshiped him; but some doubted. [18]And Jesus came and said to them, "All authority in heaven and on earth has been given to me. [19]Go therefore and make disciples of all nations, baptizing them in the name of the Father and of the Son and of the Holy Spirit, [20]and teaching them to obey everything that I have commanded you. And remember, I am with you always, to the end of the age."

Jesus' commission extended to all nations. The disciples did not have to go together into every place, but rather disperse themselves in such a manner as might best diffuse the light of the gospel to all nations. Now this plainly signifies the will of Christ—that the covenant previously made with the Jews should be canceled, and a new covenant be established to include the Gentiles. In Matthew 10 when the apostles were first sent they were sent only to the Jews and were strictly forbidden to enter the houses of Gentiles; now they were sent to all nations, beginning from Jerusalem, Judea, Samaria, and finally to all the parts of the world (Acts 1:8). Christ here displayed that salvation is offered to all, and none are excluded. The salvation to be preached is a common salvation; whoever will let him or her come.

When were they expected to carry out this task and how long was it going to take?

> [16]Now the eleven disciples went to Galilee, to the mountain to which Jesus had directed them. [17]When they saw him, they worshiped him; but some doubted. [18]And Jesus came and said to them, "All authority in heaven and on earth has been given to me. [19]Go therefore and make disciples of all nations, baptizing them in the name of the Father and of the Son and of the Holy Spirit, [20]and teaching them to obey everything

> that I have commanded you. And remember, I am with you always, to the end of the age."

Jesus' use of the words "therefore," and "always" show that the task was to be done with immediate effect. However, they were to wait first for the empowerment by the Holy Spirit before they carried on the task or mission (Acts 1:8).

Why should they engage themselves in this mission of making disciples of all nations?

> [16]Now the eleven disciples went to Galilee, to the mountain
> to which Jesus had directed them. [17]When they saw him, they
> worshiped him; but some doubted. [18]And Jesus came and
> said to them, "All authority in heaven and on earth has been
> given to me. [19]Go therefore and make disciples of all nations,
> baptizing them in the name of the Father and of the Son and
> of the Holy Spirit, [20]and teaching them to obey everything
> that I have commanded you. And remember, I am with you
> always, to the end of the age."

The main reason could be to bring a harvest of souls to Christ and to continue with Christ's mission. To expand the church, which was established on Peter the Rock. In Matthew 16:18, Jesus said this to Peter, ". . . and on this Rock I will build my church . . ." At his ascension, Jesus gave this Great Commission to make sure his church would continue to grow and live until his return. Christ's teachings transform people's lives.

What assurance did they have as they carried out this task?

> [16]Now the eleven disciples went to Galilee, to the mountain
> to which Jesus had directed them. [17]When they saw him, they

> worshiped him; but some doubted. [18]And Jesus came and said to them, "All authority in heaven and on earth has been given to me. [19]Go therefore and make disciples of all nations, baptizing them in the name of the Father and of the Son and of the Holy Spirit, [20]and teaching them to obey everything that I have commanded you. And remember, I am with you always, to the end of the age."

The motivation and promise, "I am with you" points to both the present and the future, that is, I am and I will continue to be with you (Mathew 1:23). This shows that discipleship is not a lonely road, for the risen Lord will be always be present to the end of the age."[15]

Here is the assurance Jesus gives his disciples of his spiritual presence with them in the execution of his commission: "And remember, I am with you always, to the end of the age." Here Jesus implies, "where you go I will go with you. What you do, I will do with you. What you say, I will say with you. I will be with you," but, "I Am Who I Am."

Step 3: Application

After studying a text you need to ask yourself, "So what?" This will motivate you to take action.1 John 2:5, 6 says, "But whoever obeys his word, truly in this person the love of God has reached perfection. By this we may be sure that we are in him: whoever says, "I abide in him," ought to walk just as he walked." How can you be sure that you are a disciple of Christ Jesus? If you do what Christ says and live as Christ wants, then you are a disciple. What does Christ tell us to do? 1 John 3:23 answers this question: "believe in the name of his Son Jesus Christ and love one another, just as he has commanded us." True Christian faith results in loving one another, this is the reason why John echoes that our actions give us assurance that we belong to Christ. "To walk as Jesus did" implies that we must obey Jesus Christ's teachings and follow his example of complete obedience to God and loving service to people.

Understanding the Bible is not the end goal of Bible study. It is really the beginning. It leads to application. Application is not just illustration, which only tells us how someone else handled a similar situation. It is also not just making a passage relevant, which only helps us to see that the same lessons that were true in the Bible times are true today. Application occurs only when we put God's teaching into practice so that we understand and see more of God's truth. Obeying God's Word helps us to sharpen our vision and increase our understanding. "But be doers of the word, and not merely hearers who deceive themselves. For if any are hearers of the word and not doers, they are like those who look at themselves in a mirror; for they look at themselves and, on going away, immediately forget what they were like. But those who look into the perfect law, the law of liberty, and persevere, being not hearers who forget but doers who act—they will be blessed in their doing" (James 1:22-25).

Application of God's Word is crucial. James 2:16-17 echoes that faith by itself, if it is not accompanied by action, is dead. Action demonstrates that our commitment to God is genuine. Deeds of loving service are verification of our faith in God. It calls for transformation by the renewal of one's mind and heart (Romans 12:2).

The time in the Bible study group is worthwhile and encourages openness. It helps believers to stay connected to other people in a safe environment. We need to be reminded that application is deeply personal, that is, it is unique for each individual. It is making a relevant truth a personal truth, and involves developing a strategy to live your life in harmony with the Bible. It is the biblical "how to" of life.

Making Disciples of Jesus Christ: Five Principles You Can Consider

1. Train others to help (Jesus trained the Twelve—a three year's course). Moses trained others (Exodus 18:20).
2. Teach them the Bible (Matthew 28:20, "and teach them everything I have taught you").
3. Show them the work to do (Matthew 10:1-16).
4. Transfer the anointing (Numbers 11:16, 17; Luke 9:1; 10:1, 18, 19; Acts 1:4, 5, 8).
5. Transfer the burden (Numbers 11:16-17).

What Are the Tools That Help You in Your Bible Study?

If you are sincere about studying the Bible, God will help you access the tools you need. Some possible tools are listed below.

- The Bible in your language or a language you understand;
- Different versions of the Bible to help you compare the way some of the words are used;
- A study Bible with notes at the bottom of each page to give Bible readers helpful information on the text studied;
- A Bible dictionary to give you the meaning of some biblical words that might need explanation;
- A Bible atlas to help you to locate some of the places referred to in the Bible;
- A Concordance, which lists all the words found in the Bible in alphabetical order and gives the scripture references where these words can be found;
- A pronunciation guide to help you follow the correct pronunciation of some biblical words;

- A chain reference Bible to enable you to trace all of the references on a given subject (e.g., Thomson);
- Bible commentaries that provide background information of the text.

Other Methods of Studying the Bible

You can also use methods other than the one detailed in this article to study the Bible. Two are listed below.

Studying Doctrine

In this method we study the Bible by subjects or topics, for instance: salvation, grace, justification, baptism, church, repentance, sin, atonement, etc. If a thorough doctrinal study is completed on a subject, every passage in the Bible about that subject would be analyzed, examined or studied. Effective Bible study of doctrines takes place when one takes down notes.

Studying Biblical Types

A type refers to a person or thing in the Old Testament that foreshadows a person or thing in the New Testament. For example, Moses, David, and Solomon are types of Christ. Melchizedek (Genesis 14:18-20) the high priest of the Most High God is also a type of Christ (Hebrew 7:11-28). The Passover lamb (Exodus 12:21) is also a type of Christ (Mark 14:12-16). Nothing that God does is accidental, everything the Lord has put in place is pointing to something else.

Conclusion

In this article we have established that Bible study is critical to growing effective leaders for our African churches. We have also realized that there are several benefits to those who devote themselves to Bible study. The study identified five ways in which we can take in the Bible; by hearing it, reading it, studying it, memorizing it, and meditating upon it. We have also learned that prayer is key to our Bible study. Finally, there are three steps to help us go about developing a Bible study: Bible survey, Bible analysis, and application.

Sophirina Sign is ordained clergy in The United Methodist Church in Zimbabwe East Annual Conference. She has served as a pastor of several charges, with much of her ministry in mission schools serving as chaplain.

6

Church Leadership and Management

Today we are living in a more painful and miserable society, especially in Africa. This is happening not because of poverty, but because of poor leadership. Therefore, the church in Africa needs to invest all the effort it takes to increase leadership abilities on our continent.

In one of my visits to our supporting churches in the United States, one lady asked me: "We have sent money to help you people in Africa for a hundred years, but Africa is still poor. Tell me what we need to do now so that your situation can improve?" Many Africans would answer this question by saying, "leave us alone," or "change your World Bank and IMF systems," or "stop exporting your weapons to Africa," or "stop manipulating our people," etc. While all this is true, it is not enough. Our main problem is the lack of good leadership and management. This is why learning about leadership and management is vital for our society, the church included.

Leadership and management are related, but they are not the same. Management is about doing things the "right way," but leadership is about doing the "right thing."

Management

As followers of Jesus, we are stewards, and good stewardship requires good management. Therefore, every pastor in a congregational ministry needs to develop the essential skills to manage effectively. There are three major concepts of the church that we need to understand in order to be good managers: the church as a system, the church as a business, and the pastor as manager.

The Church as a System

The church is a system because it manages people, material goods, and money. A congregation is more effective and efficient in fulfilling the purposes God intends for it when the leader manages the congregation as a system. Like the manager of a successful secular business, a managing pastor looks for the interdependence and interaction between a system's parts and the whole as well as the relationship required between three basic systemic inputs (people, facilities, and finances) to achieve desired outputs (proclamation, pastoral care, program, and mission). According to John Wimberly, pastor of Western Presbyterian Church in Washington, D.C.: a congregation must be managed as a system, which requires a plan with the pastor as the system manager.[1]

1. A systemic approach is useful to congregational management and ultimately, congregational health. Because the church is a system, every one of its aspects should be treated with the larger perspective in mind. For example, when purchasing and installing an air conditioner, one should not ignore that it would function on the same power line as computers, lights, musical instruments, and other electronics. This means that the electrical switch to be installed must be one that is capable of supporting such electrical consumption. Anxiety issues dominate systems. There are step-up issues (those that increase anxiety) and step-down issues (those that reduce anxiety). Effective managers learn how to increase step-down issues and minimize step-up issues. In church, anxiety

occurs around issues related to church finances, deferred maintenance (lack of maintenance), and personnel cost (salaries). In addition to understanding the congregational system, the pastor needs also to be aware of the societal system where they are located, because it affects them.[2]

2. For pastors, other staff, and lay leaders to effectively manage a congregational system, a congregation needs a strategic plan. A strategic plan lays out a vision for the future accompanied by broad objectives that, if accomplished, move the congregation closer to its vision. In strategic planning and implementation, the vision and objectives spring from and belong to the realm of leadership. Strategies and performance measurements are the stomping ground of managers. They are the "GPS" that guides managers in their decision-making. Leaders and managers require different but complementary skills. A leader is a visionary. She/he has a dream of what the congregation can be. A leader is a motivator and is able to mobilize church members and staff around a vision. A manager is the person who can transform that vision into reality.[3]
3. In a congregational system, the leader's role and responsibilities as manager vary, depending on the denominational polity, its membership size and constitution, and the size and configuration of its staff. As a system manager, a pastor deals with issues related to the following realities:

   - Denominational factors: the pastor must assume his/her managerial responsibility in accordance with the power given to him/her by the congregation[4]
   - Congregational and staff factors: the size of the congregation and staff determine how management responsibilities are defined and divided among the pastor, staff, and key lay people.[5]

- Managing volunteers: the management of volunteers can be sensitive, as they are not hired and therefore cannot be fired, but the pastor needs to be able to sanction them when necessary.[6]
- Getting the most from his/her team: the delegation of responsibilities by the pastor across his/her team just as Jesus did with his disciples is important.[7]

The Church as a Business

The church is a business because it manages money. John Wimberly notes that, "business is not a dirty word; it is a descriptive word. As businesses, our churches should have transparent financial operations, ethically sound personnel practices, and effective facilities management."[8] John magnifies the importance of church management in that the Christian church is the original, largest, and wealthiest multinational corporation in the world. He looks at the church as the oldest financial institution even before the existence of the World Bank or IMF. From the onset, the early church began to manage wealth and people. This is how deacons came into being in the early church; they were established to be in charge of assets and personnel management so that the Apostles could devote themselves to prayer and ministry of the Word (Acts 6:4). Then, when the church gained a lot of power thanks to the Roman hegemony, it became the first institution that handled big sums of money earned from offerings, wills, and other assets.[9]

Effective handling of finances helps a congregation to make the most out of what it has been given by God and its members so that it can accomplish its ministry goals. Church leaders should be aware of the difference between accounting and bookkeeping. It is important they receive training in accounting and financial reporting. A bookkeeper records financial events. An accountant takes the activity of the bookkeeper to a more sophisticated level where financial statements are generated for analysis and fiscal problems are solved. A comprehensive financial management program produces three kinds of reports: an income statement that displays revenues and expenses, a balance sheet that displays assets and liabilities, and a cash flow report that provides a snapshot of the current cash position.

The Pastor as Manager

It is true that pastors are trained to be leaders in the first place, but one cannot be an effective leader if he/she ignores management principles. To lead a church is to manage personnel, facilities, and finances. "The church is, first and foremost, about people," says Wimberly. Good personnel management involves three things: bringing people together to work, helping people maximize their strengths, and training and developing employees'[10] skills. To manage personnel efficiently, one must consider the following:

1. Clarifying the organizational structure: Hierarchy must be clear. Employees must know to whom they report. Generally, management of individuals by groups is a disaster.[11]
2. Managing personnel as part of the system: Just as a car cannot run simply on tires if the engine is broken, a person cannot be effective if the system has a problem.[12]
3. Aligning staff towards congregational goals: Every person must work for the same goal even if he/she takes different paths to get there. If everyone has his or her own agenda, failure is most likely to happen because an individual cannot succeed unless the system succeeds.[13]
4. Using teams to manage: No one person can do everything alone. The team concept requires a congregation and staff to shift from

individual to group responsibility. Those who are called to be leaders in the church must be team players.[14]

5. Managing through personnel policies: A good personnel policy creates the framework for healthy, ongoing discussion about how employees are to be treated by a congregation. This includes: job descriptions, performance evaluations, hiring and firing criteria, compensation packages, the right to appeal, and policies that keep good staff in place.[15]

Leadership

Leadership is the art of leading people. Leadership can be a double-edged sword: a leader must know how to meet needs of his/her followers, and at the same time empower them to do some things for themselves. To lead God's people is to help them take the next faithful step. In doing so, the leader not only does his/her job well, but also takes them where they ought to go[16]—not where they want to go—because the leader knows the "green pastures" (Psalm 23, 2), and goes in front of them.

Leadership is about change. Change is the basic principle that brings every being to existence. Change began with God. The Bible tells us that from the beginning God brought the universe into existence through change: he changed the formless earth into an organized world that we see and enjoy today (Genesis 1:2). And day after day God leads us toward the future through change. Change will continue even to the end of the time. And the One who sits on the eternal throne says in Revelation 21:5: "I am making all things new." That is why those who are called to the task of leadership must be masters of change. To be effective, the leader must be aware of the interaction between four fundamental elements: vision, team, culture, and integrity.[17]

Vision

A vision is a dream, a picture of what is possible, of a preferred future. A vision answers the question: How do I help people to walk toward the future? Vision always exists in relation to mission, but it is different from the mission itself. The mission could be defined as the thing that we exist to do—our reason for being. The vision is the next step to take toward that mission. So the mission is bigger than the vision, and the vision serves the mission. Both mission and vision cause change in God's people.

Vision is informed by the past, but aims toward the future because leadership is always about the future. God is a God of the past and the present who takes us into the future. We point to what God did for us in the past so that we can be led in the future. We cannot become what we intend to be by staying what we are now. We have to change, and change is about the future. Whatever we do and how we do it, we come back to these three elements: who we are (identity), what we do now (internal context), and the context in which we do it (external context). To draw a positive vision, one needs to consider important clues related to these elements. The right vision provides energy for other things to happen.[18]

During the early years of Christianity, Egypt and other countries in North Africa were heavily Christian countries. Some renowned theologians like St. Augustine are from North Africa. But today Egypt is 90 percent Muslim. What happened? Among other factors, Muslims cast a vision that respects the identity of the African people. When the early Christian missionaries came to Africa, they preached a gospel that obliged Africans to get rid of every traditional practice. Even playing the drum was forbidden in the church. Identity, internal context, and external context were violated. To be a Christian was understood as being cut off from one's[19] own African identity in order to embrace some foreign identity. The result is that the church was, and perhaps still is, full of people with a feeling of ambivalence. They come to church to hear the sermon on Sunday morning, but when they are sick, they go to the witch doctor. African theology has been struggling to correct this mistake for many years now.

Muslims, on the contrary, have done better than Christians in acculturating their message. The cultural values of different ethnic groups can be incorporated into the values of Islam. Muslims don't feel the obligation to separate themselves from their cultural roots. One example is that of the healing process. When a Muslim is sick he has the right to consult a marabou, a religious leader who combines both Islamic and traditional powers to obtain answers from the supernatural world. The process by which answers are obtained is divination; and divination is the main form of problem solving in African Traditional Religions.

"Where there is no vision, the people perish," (Proverbs 29:18, KJV). The leader formulates and communicates a clear vision of God's future. Although the vision must come from shared feelings, the leader is the main storyteller. If the leader doesn't tell the true story, other people will tell their own stories. And when others tell their own stories, it will result in multiple visions that will be hard to pursue at the same time. Moses had a vision of taking the children of Israel to the Promised Land (Exodus 3:1–4:17). John the Baptist had the vision of liberating peasant Israel from the bondage of Roman officials and Jewish rulers who crushed them (Matthew 3:1-12). In spite of his premature death, John's vision was carried out by Jesus. More than John, Jesus had the vision of liberating Israel not only from the slavery of earthly rulers but also from the slavery of sin. Jesus also had the vision of liberating all nations (Luke 4: 16-22). Paul likewise had the vision of taking the gospel beyond Israel's borders (Acts 22:1-21). Moses, John the Baptist, Jesus, and Paul received their visions from God and communicated them with their followers. They were the main storytellers of God's vision.

Through vision, God allows us to see beyond the visible, the barriers, and the obstacles to our mission. Thanks to the vision that God provides, we can see the invisible with the eyes of faith, and we can know the unknowable, think the unthinkable, and experience what has not yet occurred. God allows us to see signs of his kingdom. Even when things seem tough and risky, vision helps us to stay focused and fuels energy in us because the vision represents the story through which one sees reality. It gives meaning, direction, and life to God's mission.

Team

To be effective, a leader must know how to motivate those without whom the vision would not become a reality. Leadership is always about a group. One cannot be a leader of oneself. John Maxwell, an experienced leader and founder of many successful businesses in the United States says that, "he who thinks he leads, but has no followers, is only taking a walk."[20] Being a leader is not necessarily being wiser than other people, but paying attention to what is being said and what is not being said to discover where the needs are. It means to have concentration that will bring inspiration. All of us are leaders and all of us are followers depending on time and circumstances. A true leader observes what is happening and sets his or her mind to do something. An effective leader recognizes potential in others. Moses, Jesus, and Paul saw potential in their followers, and they empowered them. Empowering other leaders helps to share the burden of leadership. One of the ways to empower others is to delegate responsibility. Moses did so with the elders of Israel, Jesus with the Twelve, and Paul with his coworkers and companions.

A vision must come out of shared feelings and convictions. That is why a vision cannot be established by edict. It is an act of persuasion. It is the creation of an enthusiastic and dedicated commitment to a vision because it is right for the time, right for the organization, and right for the people who are working in it.

An effective leader builds a strong team around him- or herself that helps to implement the vision. A good leader knows that one can't do it alone. We all need the support and the wisdom of other people. Moses had Aaron as spokesperson from the onset of his leadership. On Jethro's counsel, Moses appointed other leaders among the people to share the leadership burden with him. Jesus likewise had a team of 12 disciples that he trained and sent out to share the gospel. Paul also followed the same pattern. He had a team of coworkers and companions that were of great help to him. He did not do it alone. Moses, Jesus, and Paul recognized that success comes from a team effort. This is what Norman Cohen means when he affirms, "Leaders must acknowledge that they cannot control and run everything. What ultimately makes leaders successful, among many crucial traits, is their humility, even as they embody the highest ideals and standards of the group."[21]

Culture

Professor Lovett Weems of Wesley Theological Seminary in Washington, D.C., affirms this Merriam Webster definition: "Culture is the integrated pattern of human behavior that includes thought, speech, action, and artifacts, or values that are shared by the people in a group and that tend to persist over time even when group membership changes." He goes on to say, "It is simply the way we do things."[22] Once we have the vision, we must build the team. The next step is to know how that vision can come alive in the culture, because otherwise things will never happen. In order to succeed it is important to be a team that understands the culture, because the culture carries the vision.

People resist change because they feel that their culture is challenged. Habits, values, and attitudes—even dysfunctional ones—are part of one's identity. To change the way people see and do things is to challenge how they define themselves. During one of his lectures on Church Leadership Excellency at Wesley Theological Seminary in Washington, D.C., Lovett told attendees that an effective leader helps people to "live their life in a new way of thinking instead of force them think their way in a new way of living."[23] I remember asking him to repeat this phrase so that I could jot it down; because I did not understand it the first time he said it. It's not always necessary to change things formally, you can just say: "can we try this for two weeks?" and see what happens. If it works, then you can continue, otherwise you can stop it and find other ways. It takes time for people to adapt to change, especially when it is adaptive rather than technical. Technical change is simple, but adaptive change is complex because it is emotional. For instance we can change the worship style overnight, that's a technical change; but the transition in people's minds will take a while because it is adaptive change. That's why we don't have to force people when it comes to change, we must be patient.

Integrity

Integrity is critical for a leader because it is the key, not only to his or her own credibility, but also to the credibility of the organization. Integrity is then an essential element of church leadership. What is at stake is not so much the public image of a profession, but the effectiveness of ministry.

The effectiveness of leadership depends on the integrity of the leader and community. First, concerning the integrity of the leader, the question is: are we willing to "wear the vision" that we have stated? In other words: are we willing to be the living example of the vision? Otherwise there would be inconsistency. What the leader says and what he/she does must be aligned. A leader's credibility and the trust that people have in their leader are the capital of his or her leadership. Second, there are three kinds of core values related to the integrity of the community:

- Proclaimed value: what people say they are;
- Perceived value: what other people say they are;
- Produced value: what the ideal should be.

When what we claim is not what we really are, then we need to address the issue and work to obtain agreement in our core values. Otherwise we lose our integrity by continuing to claim what we are not.

Signs of Genuine Leadership

Leaders must be able to face the challenges that come with their role. Skill, knowledge, and talent are not sufficient to make a good leader. A leader needs to be spiritually, emotionally, and physically balanced. It is only when a leader knows how to hold all of these values in check that he/she will be able to make a real impact.

Leaders Exercise Shepherd Leadership

A shepherd is an image of a loving God who cares for his flock. In ancient Israel, sheep were very important and a shepherd was a metaphor of honor. Sheep were meant for wool. Sheep also provided meat to eat. To offer a sheep to a guest was to honor him/her. Sheep shearing time was a time for fellowship.

Just as the loving God takes care of his people, a shepherd leader meets the needs of his or her followers. Shepherd leadership is a matter of head and hand and heart; it is a way of thinking and doing and being. While in the thinking mode, shepherd leaders endeavor to think, make plans, and discover needs. In the doing mode, they act to meet those needs and demonstrate compassion through their actions. In the being mode, they establish contact and relate with followers because, "a hallmark of shepherd leadership is both the ability and the willingness to see life from the perspective of the follower."[24]

Shepherd leaders go out and see what happens to their followers. In Exodus 2:13, Moses leaves his comfort zone to be with his brothers and sisters. He sees two Hebrews fighting, and he tries to bring peace among them. Here Moses is reaching out to see his fellows.

Sheep need to be drawn and not driven, that means to go in front of them. However, there is tension between driving and drawing, because you don't need to give a choice to the sheep all the time. A shepherd knows where the pastures are and drives the sheep there. They need to be driven when they take a wrong direction. In Numbers 16, Korah, Dathan, and Abiram led a strike against Moses. They wanted to lead the people back to Egypt, but Moses knew that that was a wrong move. He did not negotiate at all. He stood firm.

A shepherd leader is willing to take risks. From the onset when he was yet in Pharaoh's palace, Moses took the risk of seeking justice for an Israelite who was abused by an Egyptian taskmaster. This situation caused him to flee to Median where he had yet to face permanent dangers inherent to keeping sheep in the wilderness. Then God asked him to go back to Egypt to face Pharaoh's wrath for killing the Egyptian taskmaster. Even when Moses succeeded to get the children of Israel out of Egypt, he continued to face risks—any time the Israelites encountered a problem that seemed to have no solution, they rushed to Moses as a mob ready to lynch him (Exodus 15:22-27; 16:1-4; Numbers 20:1-13). The leader should decide which risks are worth taking and which ones are not.

Leaders Can Experience Crisis, Loss, Struggle, and Pain

Leaders are also vulnerable human beings. They can experience crisis, loss, struggle, and pain. When the time is right, leaders should feel free to mourn and let others mourn, too. It is not right to suppress people from mourning. King David mourned for his son Absalom. Jesus mourned for his friend Lazarus. Pain and mourning are natural human emotions. They humble us and bring healing. Grief moves people from abundance to fairness. Grief is also a sharp tool to cut through numbness and self-deception. Weeping is a sign of passion, and tears are a sign of solidarity and pain. Even God weeps for the people (Jeremiah 9:10, 17). Jesus also wept for Jerusalem (Matthew 23:37). Weeping provides release and brings newness. Jesus had compassion for Jerusalem. "Compassion" in Hebrew comes from the word rechamin, which means womb. So to have compassion is to be touched in the bottom of the womb. It is necessary then, to cultivate the culture to lament and grieve when necessary. It is not right to prevent people from being emotional.

Because leaders can experience crisis, loss, struggle, and pain, they need mentors who can watch over them and encourage them in times of bitterness and despair. Even a great King like David had Joab as mentor.

Leaders acknowledge that faith in the Bible includes core testimonies and counter-testimonies. Core testimonies are positive affirmations concerning God. Counter-testimonies are statements that come out of our experience and contradict who we say God is. Examples of core testimonies: God lives, God is holy, God forgives, God saves, God heals, God hears, God blesses, God accompanies, etc. Examples of counter-testimonies: God, why? God, do you care? God, do you hear me? God, how long? etc. In Job's story his friends give a counter-testimony and God provides the core testimony. In good leadership, there is room to hold core and counter-testimonies in tension. It is not healthy to suppress the counter-testimonies when people bring them up. Letting them speak about them is a way to introduce healing.

In Jacob's story, he sends his wives, children, and servants in front and stays alone at the Jabbok River for self-examination (Genesis 32:24-32). The wrestling with God at night indicates that Jacob was also wrestling with himself in order to try to give a meaning to his life. Then, he names the place Peniel (God's face). Here, Jacob is telling the story of his beginning. One of the ways for leaders to perform self-examination consists of recalling their own stories—going back to the beginning to determine what called them to ministry, why they were so eager about it, and what happened next.

Leaders Are Set Apart

Leadership necessarily sets leaders apart from others. There is a potential cost to relationship when one answers the call to leadership. Sometimes, being set apart brings suffering and pain. Moses suffered. He was obliged to flee from Egypt because he tried to help his fellow Israelites. In the wilderness people challenged his authority in spite of all the wonders he had performed. People did not have respect for Moses even when he was mourning his deceased sister Miriam. But the most painful episode of Moses' leadership was that he was denied entry to the Promised Land after all the hardships he had endured. For David's story, he was separated from his friend Jonathan and his wife Michal because of Saul's anger so that he could become the leader he ought to be. Jesus suffered as well. He and his followers lived a life of wandering charismatics. Jesus had no home. He was separated from his biological family. Jesus was constantly attacked by religious authorities and he finally paid with his life for the sake of leadership. Paul is no exception. He ran into trouble with the church in Jerusalem because of the gospel, and he became the enemy of many. Five times the Jews gave Paul 39 blows (2 Corinthians 11:24), and he was imprisoned in Rome—all for the sake of leadership.

Being set apart can cause pain and risk. But even as such it is worth it, because leaders serve others and get opportunities to express love to them. The most important thing is that while leaders are set apart, they stay connected to God. This is what Lewis A. Park, Professor at Wesley Theological Seminary in Washington, D.C., means when he affirms that "to be set apart for leadership is not to be isolated and lonely, but a call to recognize our connection to God as the defining element in our lives."[25] Thanks to the connection to God, one makes appropriate choices of words, tones, and actions. This connection also prepares one to adapt to different circumstances. It is this connection to God that allowed David to use the holy bread for secular purposes (1 Samuel 21:3-6) and dared live with the Philistines, Israel's enemies (1 Samuel 27).

Leaders Know Themselves

A genuine leader assesses his/her strengths and weaknesses and acts accordingly. Jonathan and David were best friends. Jonathan gave his royal vestments to David, which symbolized that he was giving his royalty to David (1 Samuel 18:4). Then when Jonathan's father tried to kill David, he helped David escape. This made Saul angry with his son. Why did Jonathan act this way knowing that helping David to escape meant risking losing his own royalty at David's benefit? Because Jonathan saw leadership qualities in David that he didn't see within himself. When a leader sees qualities in other people he/she recognizes them and encourages them.

In Moses' case, he assessed his strengths and weaknesses and realized that he was not worthy when God called him. So, he replied to God: "Who am I that I should go to Pharaoh, and bring the Israelites out of Egypt?" (Exodus 3:11). One of the genuine characteristics of leadership is to know oneself very well. To know oneself, a leader needs time for self-examination. Leaders can make two mistakes: they can focus on themselves and forget others, or they can focus on the ministry and forget to get in touch with themselves. That is why they need time for reaching out and time for withdrawing for self-examination. Even Jesus had to withdraw sometimes. To do this, leaders need humility and self-confidence.

Leaders Know that Leadership Grows Over Time

John Maxwell calls this leadership principle "the law of process." He writes: "everyone has the potential, but it isn't accomplished overnight.

It requires perseverance. And you absolutely cannot ignore the law of process. Leadership doesn't develop in a day."[26] It requires perseverance, discipline, and commitment. International football stars or those of any other sport don't become famous overnight. They work on their skills for years before attaining the top level. Likewise, God prepares leaders step by step. The burning bush (snei) that Moses saw and the Mount Sinai are the same word in Hebrew. It means that God was preparing Moses since the onset. God prepared him through the process of being the shepherd of Jethro's sheep to become the greatest leader that Israel had ever known. David also went through the same process: God prepared him from being the shepherd of his father's sheep to the king of Israel.

Just as they know that leadership grows over time, leaders also recognize and communicate that redemption comes in stages. In Exodus 6:6, this process is shown by the use of different expressions: "I will free you" (physical freedom); then "I will deliver you" (spiritual freedom); finally "I will stretch my arm" (bound to God).[27]

Leaders Exercise Servant Leadership

The true measure of leadership is service and sacrifice: "For the Son of Man came not to be served but to serve, and to give his life as a ransom for many" (Mark 10:45). Leadership is not about glory and honor. When we look at Moses, Jesus, and Paul's stories, we realize that they were more servants than masters. Their priority was to serve others.

Following in the steps of Moses, Jesus, and Paul, church leaders today must have a strong concern for the poor, the marginalized, the "least of these" (Matthew 25:40, 45). While it is right to say that the church must care for the poor, it should also be said that the church must challenge the rich, so that it can have the means to care for the poor.

To serve is also to bring reconciliation. In this world of hatred and conflicts, church leaders must develop a ministry of reconciliation because, "in Christ God was reconciling the world to himself, not counting their trespasses against them, and entrusting the message of reconciliation to us" (2 Corinthians 5:19). Moreover, dialogue must be added to reconciliation for a complete action of healing of our corrupted world, because many are using the religion to express their distorted political ambitions. Religious leaders must learn and promote humility by teaching not to retaliate especially where many cry out for revenge at all costs. However, the problem is that of knowing what the just measure between love and justice is.

Leaders Are Good Communicators

An effective communicator expresses ideas with clarity. He/she is understandable and at the same time, is a good listener, influential, and persuasive (not manipulative). One of the ways in which Jesus excelled in good communication was through parables. Jesus used parables because they belonged to the rhetoric of his culture, they were full of meaning and interesting for the hearers, and they called for action.

Following Jesus' model a church leader must be a good communicator. The leader is the chief communication officer, the chief storyteller. If he/she doesn't tell the true story, people will tell their own stories. The leader's message should always call for a decision that offers a response to the person who listens. For example: if a leader preaches on forgiveness, he/she should ask listeners to forgive each other. It is important to stay on the message, remain fresh and natural, and not try to impress people in an unnatural way.

Leaders are Mentors and Models

A leader must be a mentor and model, just as Jesus was for his disciples and Paul for his coworkers and companions. Paul wrote in 1 Corinthians

11:1, "Be imitators of me, as I am of Christ." Imitation is the sincerest form of discipleship. Since there was no school, imitating the master was the only way of learning. So for Paul to say, "imitate me," was not a form of arrogance. Jesus' disciples also learned by imitation. Thus we read in Luke 11:1: "He was praying in a certain place, and after he had finished, one of his disciples said to him, "Lord, teach us to pray . . ."

Imitation of the master by the disciple assures continuity. We see this principle of continuity in Jesus' relationship with John the Baptist, then with his disciples. Jesus picked up where John had left off: some of John's disciples became Jesus' disciples. But there was also some discontinuity; Jesus did not baptize people as John did. In prison, John sent a message to Jesus to ask if he was the messiah because he saw some discontinuity between Jesus and him. Jesus had a group that lived with him that he taught. He sent them out and gave them responsibility. There was a sense that he was already working on what must come after him. That also was about continuity. Jesus did not simply teach them by words, he also taught them through action. For instance, he washed their feet and told them to do the same (John 13:1-17). Here Jesus modeled the action. Church leaders must also teach by being the examples of the change we need to become.

Leaders Assume a Prophetic Role

A prophet is someone who speaks on God's behalf and one who warns and pronounces judgment as well. Jesus is the best example of both aspects of the prophet. He issued a series of blessings in the famous Beatitudes (Matthew 5:1-12), but he also pronounced seven woes in Matthew 23.

Church leaders, as prophets, have a double task: that of offering an expectation into which we might live today and that of pronouncing warning and judgment against evil. This is one aspect that needs to be more fully developed in church ministry on the African continent as a whole, not just in our church. African institutions, including churches, are suffering because of the lack of prophetic message. No one dares to speak up to denounce abuses committed by authorities because of fear. To take just one example, when I travel to visit churches located in the regions out of the capital city, I would drive for more than five hours to cover just less than 100 miles because the road is almost impassable. But on the map, that road is tiled. People who received the money to tile the road have used it for their personal needs. Everyone knows about that, but there is no punishment because everyone in the government does the same, and there is no one who dares to speak up about it. In our churches in Africa, things are no better. Some church leaders use big sums of money for purposes other than those for which they were destined. To succeed to do so, they appoint people of their ethnic groups to work close to them, or they choose people whom they know who cannot challenge them in any shape or form.

Conclusion

Leadership and management are two different, but complementary, things. One cannot exist without the other. Leadership is the art of leading people by meeting their needs and taking them where they ought to go—not where they want to go. Management is about administrating people, material goods, and money. Both concepts relate to each other. To be effective in their work, leaders must be aware of the interaction between four major concepts that determine people's lives: vision, team, culture, and integrity. God calls church leaders, not to be successful, but to be fruitful. For this reason, leaders must be those who:

- exercise shepherd leadership;
- experience and accept crisis, loss, struggle, and pain;
- are set apart;

- know themselves;
- know that leadership grows over time, not in a day;
- exercise servant leadership;
- are good communicators;
- are mentors and models for others; and
- assume a prophetic role.

Nkemba Ndjungu is a ministerial member of the United Methodist Annual Conference in Southern Congo. He holds a Master of sacred theology degree from Boston University School of Theology and a Doctorate in ministry from Wesley Theological Seminary. He has served as a district superintendent in the Democratic Republic of Congo, and as the mission superintendent in Senegal for 10 years. Since 2008 he has been serving as mission superintendent of the Cameroon Mission Initiative. He has been involved from the beginning of the Academies for Evangelization and Church Growth.

7

The Impact of Religious Communities in the 2011 Electoral Process in the Democratic Republic of the Congo: A Case Study of the Kamina Community

In recent years, many African countries have been struggling with the transfer of political power through democratic elections. This has often led to killings, violence, and civil wars. Sub-Saharan Africa has been the most affected by electoral violence. Countries such as Côte d'Ivoire, Nigeria, Kenya, Zimbabwe, and the Democratic Republic of Congo (DR Congo), have been caught between the challenges of terminating war and beginning a process of democratization. Although religion has not surfaced as a major drive for electing candidates in DR Congo and Zimbabwe, it has had played a role in Côte d'Ivoire, Nigeria, and to some extent Kenya, where elections were about choosing between Christian and Muslim candidates. In Nigeria for instance, the April 2011presidential elections spurred several cases of violent conflicts between Muslims and Christians, which led to the killing and displacement of many people, especially women and children. A close look at the 2011 Congolese electoral politics suggested that religion had an impact on the choice of most candidates. Religious demographics and identity are factors that have been affecting elections in a number of African countries. In DR Congo, the tension is between the Roman Catholic Church and the Churches of Christ in Congo (ECC), which is composed of a significant number of Protestant churches including The United Methodist Church. Because of this dynamic, it is not surprising that in the 2006 electoral process, the head of the independent electoral commission was a Roman Catholic priest and in the 2011 electoral process, the head of electoral commission was a Protestant pastor from the Nouvelle Eglise Methodiste (New Methodist Church), a new denomination which broke away from The United Methodist Church in the Central Congo Episcopal area.

This article seeks to engage in a discussion about the impact of religion on the 2011 electoral process in Kamina, DR Congo, which is a post-conflict religious setting. Because the DR Congo, in general and Kamina, in particular, has been one of the most conflict-ridden areas on the continent of Africa, this article will examine the role that religion has played in peace and conflict, and how it contributed to peaceful free and fair 2011 elections. The ambivalent character of religion in regard to stopping or causing violent conflicts is critical to the discussion.

This article will be framed around the following thematic areas: religious presence in Kamina; approaches to defining religion; the study of elections, religion, and the 2011 elections in Kamina; and recommendations.

Religious Presence in Kamina and DR Congo

The statistics below show the diversity that exists in DR Congo.

- The population is estimated at about 75,507,308 (July 2013 estimate).[1]
- Nearly 80 percent of the Congolese population is Christian.
- The Lubas who occupy Kamina and most of the North Katanga area are among the largest ethnic groups. The population of Kamina is estimated at about 250,000 people, this includes those who live in the remote areas outside of Kamina as well.
- There are more than 250 spoken languages that reflect the cultural diversity of the DR Congo.[2]

The religious presence in DR Congo is represented by the following statistics:

- African Traditional Religion: 10 percent;
- Roman Catholics: 50 percent;
- Protestant: 30 percent (including Indigenous Christianity or Kimbanguists); and
- Islam: 10 percent.[3]

There is a significant presence of Christians in DR Congo in general, and Kamina in particular. However, in spite of this significant religious presence DR Congo has gone through many bloody conflicts since its independence. Therefore, the question that needs to be asked is what role has religion played, especially Christianity in the quest for peace and development in Kamina and DR Congo as a whole? It appears that the political establishment, especially under the Mobutu regime, has manipulated religion, Christianity in particular, for political motivations.[4]

Under the Mobutu regime, there was strong pressure from the Roman Catholic Church through Cardinal Malula who called for Mobutu to put an end tyranny. In response, Mobutu encouraged the creation of "L'Eglise du Christ au Congo" (ECC), leading to its establishment in 1970. The ECC united more than 64 member Protestant churches in the DR Congo. During the same year, the Rev. Dr. Bokeleyale was elected as president of the ECC. President Mobutu, who initiated the creation of this ecumenical body, helped this new organization to get funding from various external partners. This new body stood as a power block and it was a device through which Mobutu could control the Protestant churches against the pressure from the Roman Catholic Church. After Laurent Kabila overthrew Mobutu in 1997, the ECC was used again to uphold Laurent Kabila in power before he was assassinated in 2001. With the coming of Joseph Kabila, the ECC was useful for the new government's[5] drive for national dialogue, reconciliation, and a move towards a peace agreement and eventually a cease-fire. Once again the ECC did not have its own agenda for peace and reconciliation but adopted the Congolese government's. It is not surprising then, that religious identity played a role in the formation of the Congolese electoral independent commission whose leadership was given first to a Roman Catholic priest and currently to a Protestant pastor.[6]

Defining Religion

The following includes various definitions of religion in the context of elections.

"Religion is indeed powerful medicine; it should be administered prudently, selectively, and deliberately . . . religion is the human response to a reality perceived as sacred . . . religion as interpreter of the sacred, discloses and celebrates the transcendent source and significance of human existence."[7] For the nearly 73 percent of the Congolese population who are considered Christian, there seem to be agreement about who is "the sacred." Belief in one God and salvation through Jesus Christ is at the core of both Protestant and Roman Catholic doctrines. It is important to note that the diversity of cultures already present among the Congolese population is expressed through the different ways in which people respond to the sacred. The Lubas, the majority ethnic group in Kamina, are known as people who sing, dance, and experience prophecy. They have the tendency to embrace Christianity in the same way whether they are Roman Catholic or Protestant. In this regard, Appleby argues that "the encounter with the sacred is always a dialectical experience of mystery (mysterium): the feeling of dread evoked by its overpowering and uncontrollable presence (tremendum): comes bound up together with feelings of awe, wonder, and fascination (fascinans)." Religion then, Appleby argues, "encompasses the range of diverse responses to this dialectical experience of the sacred."[8]

What is interesting in the election period is that for some a political charismatic leader is perceived as an individual who God has called to lead the country. For example, for the Kasai people in DR Congo see Etienne Tshisekedi as someone that God has called to lead the country. In fact, several Pentecostal churches in the Kasai region or those led by Kasai pastors, provide him with some prophetic backing. Similarly, the Luba people in Kamina, see Joseph Kabila as someone that God has called to lead the country. It should be noted that during the campaign some political leaders would[9] "consult traditional religious leaders such as juju men or malams to assist them with spiritual support particularly during election campaigns and ultimately help them win elections."[10]

In the case of Ghana, a Pentecostal pastor by the name of T.B Joshua is known to have prophesized to President Mills that he would win the 2009 elections. "Consequently, in his capacity as special spiritual adviser, Joshua is purported to wield a lot of influence over the president. All this is played out in the Ghanaian public sphere, indicating the continued pivotal role religion plays in the Ghanaian body polity."[11]

The fact that some political charismatic leaders are perceived by some as "sacred," complicates elections. In such cases it is not surprising to experience post-electoral violence, especially when one leader or the other failed to win. Such violence is significant when it has a religious motivation.

Religion, then, becomes very ambiguous as humans respond differently. In this regard Appleby argues, "from a religious point of view, then, living with ambiguity is the consequence of the distance between the infinite God and the contingent human being."[12] Religion is also a yearning for transcendence, for moving and reaching beyond the mundane, the spatial and the temporal, the physical and contingent.

The fact that religion can produce peace and violence at the same time makes religion ambivalent. "Ambivalence describes the primordial state of religious consciousness but not its mature expression."[13] In the context of elections, religion can either be an opportunity to bring about peaceful free and fair elections or a source of electoral violence.

The Study of Elections

The practice of elections began within aristocratic societies when people had to choose leaders from among several candidates. In this setting, each individual was given an equal chance to attain a higher social position. It should be noted that accessing equal opportunities was considered a key element by democracy's[14] founders. In the case of Kamina, Christians, Muslims, or Traditionalists must be given equal opportunities to choose a candidate. The Roman Catholic majority must not impose their choice on the members of the ECC. "Elections signify choice and choice may be combined with electoral operations."[15] They give people an opportunity to choose their own leaders regardless of religion or denomination. "Elections are central to theory and practice of constitutional democracy"[16] and the fairness and freedom of elections is very critical. That is why all religions must make it a noble mission to work for free and fair elections as a way to usher in a new genuine democratic society.

Even if elections are often regarded as a peaceful means towards conflict resolution within democracy, they also come with a certain dose of violence. This implies that there is a strong dilemma between elections and violence. Sometimes elections silence guns, other times they create bullets. For instance, in Namibia the 1989 elections ended 20 years of war and the same scenario occurred in the 1990 elections in Nicaragua and the 1991 elections in El Salvador. However, in the case of the 1993 elections in the Republic of Congo, a civil war erupted after the results were announced and the forces of General Denis Sassou Nguesso overthrew the then elected president Pascal Lissuba. The 2010 elections in Côte[17] d'Ivoire were expected to bring about peace and stability after a long transition, but instead led to civil war in the streets of Abidjan. Religion played a role as people had to choose between a Christian and a Muslim candidate.

In a post-conflict context, elections are caught in between the challenge of war termination and that of democratization This is the case in Kamina, where elections are still seen as a way out of violent conflicts. According to Rapoport and Weimberg, "in case of civil wars, elections are accepted because the parties decide that they cannot win the military struggle or that winning costs too much."[18] Furthermore, they note, "because elections are crucial ingredients of modern democracy, good democrats will be dismayed to learn that elections are often associated with outbursts of violence."[19] If violence is expected then, religious communities in Kamina must take measures to prevent or deal with the violence. There needs to be an ongoing dialog that leads people and all stakeholders to create an environment that is conducive for peaceful elections.

Rapoport and Weimberg summarize the election-violence debate by indicating that the moment elections results are announced is very critical in terms of whether they will trigger violence. They argue that, "normally, post elections violence occurs when results are announced but issues may explode later."[20] This clearly shows that the media have a significant role to play in ensuring peaceful elections. In this regard, religious communities must engage the Congolese media as well to encourage ethically motivated practices rather than political ones. This seems to be a very sensitive area because almost every major politician seems to have his or her hand in the media. Religious communities in Kamina, and in DR Congo in general, called upon the parliament and the national electoral commission to have regulations, which would conduct the media during the 2011 elections.

It is very difficult to know when violence will occur. In general, violence can occur before, during, or after elections. Though called electoral violence, it may also take place sometime after the elections. This violence can take other dimensions when it is done in the name of religion, which is why religious leaders must place themselves on the side of peace. Because elections are capable of bringing about violent conflicts, it is critical to analyze the dynamics between religion and conflicts.

Religion, Elections, and Conflicts

The post-9/11 era escalated the already hot debate concerning the impact of religion in violent conflicts, which has an effect on an elected official's religious community. Regarding the relationships between religion and conflicts, there are crucial questions that remain without answers: "which conditions cause religion to escalate conflicts or contribute to peace? What is the relative weight of religion in conflict relative to other (political or economic) factors? Through which mechanisms does religion translate into escalation or de-escalation?"[21] Bearing in mind the difficulty to respond to the above questions, Matthias and Alexander suggest that there are at least four aspects as regard to the role of religion in civil conflicts, which deserve to be considered.[22]

Whereas earlier works in the field focus on the escalating effects of religion, the role of religion in conflicts is principally ambiguous. In other words,[23] "in a given setting and at a certain point in time religion may incite violence; in other circumstances it may contribute to peace or prevent violence from emerging."[24]

In the process of trying to identify why religion is ambivalent, two dimensions have to be differentiated: "the direction and the magnitude of religions' effects on conflicts. Some factors might influence the probability that religions have an escalating or de-escalating effect in a given setting. However, these factors might not influence whether religions will actually be able to have an escalating or de-escalating impact on the course of the conflict."[25] According to Matthias and Alexander, religious factors that may have an influence on how religion impacts peace and conflict can be articulated through the following five levels:

1. "Demographic religious structures and dynamics, that is, the share and relative number of people affiliated with different religions or denominations in a given society as well as changes in these structures."[26] As indicated, in Kamina there are Roman Catholics, Protestants, traditionalists, Muslims, and other religions.
2. "The content and intensity of religious identities (as social identity) as well as their relationship to other identity markers such as ethnicity or region."[27] This is a very interesting point as it is expressed in the Kamina community where most people who are Lubas will identify themselves as Protestants and see themselves as "I ba mulao,"[28] or sons and daughters of promises. Therefore, they are called to lead in all aspects of life.
3. "Religious or theological ideas such as values, commandments, and beliefs, as well as their interpretation."[29]
4. "The characteristics of religious organizations and institutions."[30]
5. "The (possibly idiosyncratic) traits of individual religious leaders."[31]

There are, of course, other variables that affect the course of peace and conflicts.

Religion offers opportunity for peace and conflict transformation in an electoral context. Roman Catholic and ECC religious leaders in Kamina worked together with the government, the national electoral commission, the media, and other stakeholders to ensure peaceful free and fair elections in 2011. Even when there were issues between different parties in the course of elections, religious leaders had the opportunity to use their skills to mediate the parties and help them find durable solutions.

"At the heart of peacemaking is conflict transformation, the replacement of violent with nonviolent means of settling disputes," writes Appleby. Since electoral violence was inevitable in DR Congo, religious leaders had the opportunity to engage the parties in conflict transformation. In this regard, Appleby stresses that conflict transformation offers three dimensions, which are conflict management, conflict resolution, and structural reform.[32,33]

In conflict management, religious communities and leaders in Kamina had the opportunity to develop effective measures to prevent or contain deadly conflicts by articulating the problems that create conflicts. Churches and religious communities in Kamina mobilized social forces capable of addressing any potential electoral conflict.[34]

In conflict resolution, religious leaders and communities in Kamina deployed systemic efforts to combat prejudice and ethno-religious hatred through dialogue and education in order to serve the goals of conflict transformation. In this regard, Appleby argues that[35] "faith can form a powerful connection between adversaries or mediators and one or more parties they seek to reconcile."[36]

It should be noted that in a pragmatic way, various religious leaders of Kamina engaged the community in voter education through seminars on elections. The first series of seminars was held in April 2011 in Kamina and the second was held in Kinshasa at the end of August 2011. The seminars on elections received financial support from the General Board of Church and Society of The United Methodist Church. This effort made by The United Methodist Church was followed by various similar initiatives put together by other faith communities.

During the 2011 elections in Kamina, The United Methodist Church and other faith communities made sure every citizen exercised his or her civic right to vote. Religious leaders in Kamina had the opportunity to make use of the three modes of religious conflict transformation as proposed by Appleby, which are crisis, saturation, and intervention.

In the crisis mode, religious charismatic leadership of the Kamina community, were catalysts for the marshaling of social resources and personal commitment. In the saturation mode, religious communities of Kamina were inspired by the actions taken in Northern Ireland, where the peace advocates operated at several levels of religion and society and persisted through decades of continuous activity and became part of the institutional landscape. Finally, in the intervention mode religious leaders in Kamina mediated some dialogue between warring parties when they failed to agree on the elections results. It is important to note that religious leaders in Kamina were proactive in their engagement efforts through conversations with all presidential candidates, urging them to commit themselves to the election outcomes. The United Methodist Church leadership in Kamina and throughout DR Congo played a positive role in ensuring peaceful free and fair elections. It is in this regard that Bishop Ntambo, Bishop Katembo, and Bishop Yemba were engaged at various levels of the community on issues of elections. This great example was followed by various local pastors and church leaders who put a lot of time and resources in building capacities of their members on the issues of elections. The involvement of religious communities in future elections and vital issues of any African nation will have to be part of mission and evangelism efforts.[37,38]

Electing one candidate over another should not be about religion or ethnicity, but instead about freely choosing a candidate who responds to one's aspiration and that of the community. It should also not be about choosing a Roman Catholic or an ECC member. Religion should not be the major deciding factor in any elections in Kamina, DR Congo, as well as in other countries in Africa.

Appleby offers the peacemaking side of religion, which is critical to creating a conducive environment for free and fair elections. The institutional Roman Catholic Church and the ECC must not push for their agendas, but instead they should allow the Congolese people, as people of God, to let their will and aspirations be expressed through the ballots. As religious institutions, it is in their prophetic mandate to accompany the Congolese people throughout the electoral process. It is important to affirm the positive role that Kamina religious leaders, whether Methodists, Muslims, or Roman Catholics, played during the 2011 elections in DR

Congo. Kamina religious leaders provided the tools that the community needed to ensure peaceful, free, and fair elections. These religious leaders have been able to place themselves in the middle of the village as chaplains for the common good. Furthermore, they closely engaged with the media, the national electoral commission and provided electoral oversights throughout the country. Following the results, a group of religious leaders continued to have conversations with various candidates, urging them to accept the will of the people without pushing their sympathizers to acts of violence. At a national level, Bishop David Yemba served that purpose very well by representing The United Methodist Church in the mediating group of religious leaders. For future elections, it is important that The United Methodist Church continue to put forward programs that will enable the community to go through an electoral process without violence.

Mande Muyombo, originally from the Democratic Republic of Congo, is the assistant general secretary for Justice and Relationships for the General Board of Global Ministries of The United Methodist Church. He is also a board member for Africa University and the International Association of Methodist Schools, Colleges, and Universities. Prior to his work at Global Ministries, Muyombo served as the president of Kamina Methodist University in DR Congo.

Resources

Almond, Gabriel A., R. Scott Appleby, and Emmanuel Sivan. Strong Religion: The Rise of Fundamentalisms Around the World. Chicago: Chicago University Press, 2003.

Appleby, R. Scott. The Ambivalence of the Sacred: Religion, Violence, and Reconciliation. Lanham, MD: Rowman & Littlefield Publishers, 2000.

Congolese National Ministry of Planning, 2005 Report

Muyombo, Mande. The Role of the Church in Resolving the Mai-Mai Conflict in North Katanga in the DR Congo. Mutare, Zimbabwe: Africa University, 2006.

Basedau, Matthias and Alexander De Juan, The Ambivalence of the Sacred in Africa: The Impact of Religion on Peace and Conflict in Sub-Saharan Africa. German Institute of Global and Area Studies. GIGA Research Programme: Violence, Power and Security, March 2008.

Okyerefo, Michael Perry Kweku, et al. Religion as a Tool in Strengthening the Democratic Process in Ghana. University of Ghana, June 2011.

Tshilembalemba, Mukenge. Culture and Customs of the Congo. Westport, CT: Greenwood Press, 2002.

Rapoport, David C. and Leonard Weimberg. The Democratic Experience and Political Violence. London: Frank Cass, 2001.

Endnotes

Chapter 1

1 *The General Secretary's Report to the Eighth Assembly of the World Council of Churches*, Harare, Zimbabwe, December 3-4, 1998.
2 "World Population Data Sheet 2013," Population Reference Bureau, September 2013, http://www.prb.org/Publications/Datasheets/2013/2013-world-population-data-sheet/data-sheet.aspx.
3 David J. Bosch, *Transforming Mission*, (Maryknoll, New York: Orbis Books, 1997), 411.
4 *The Struggle Continues, Official Report, Third Assembly, All Africa Conference of Churches*, (Nairobi: 1975), 34.
5 Paul Gifford, *African Christianity*, (Bloomington: Indiana University Press, 1998), 63.
6 Ibid.
7 Ibid.
8 Unless otherwise noted, the 1984 New International Version of the Bible is used in this article.
9 *Rand McNally Bible Atlas*, (New York: Rand McNally & Company, 1952), 55.
10 Ibid., 57.
11 Norman K. Gottwald, *A Light to the Nations*, (New York: Harper & Row, Publishers, 1959), 230.
12 *The NIV Study Bible*, (Grand Rapids: Zondervan, 1995), 1081.
13 Ibid.
14 *Oxford Dictionary of the Bible*, (Oxford: OUP, 1996), 305.
15 John Wesley Zwomunondiita Kurewa, *An African Pilgrimage on Evangelism* (Nashville: Abingdon Press, 2011), 71ff.
16 Used with permission.
17 *Journal of the Rhodesia Annual Conference of the Methodist Church*, 1953, 158.
18 Philip S. Watson, *The Message of the Wesleys*, (New York: The Macmillan Company, 1964), 39.
19 *The Works of John Wesley*, Vol. 8, 472.
20 Watson, *The Message of the Wesleys*, 35.
21 Rupert E. Davies, *Methodism*, (London: Epworth Press, 2003), 86.
22 Davies, *Methodism*, 87.
23 Ibid.
24 Philip S. Watson, *The Message of the Wesleys*, 39.
25 George G. Hunter, *The Apostolic Congregation*, (Nashville: Abingdon Press, 2009), 8.
26 *Ibid.*, 6.

27 *The Works of John Wesley*, Vol. VIII, 472.
28 *Oxford Dictionary of the Bible*, 318.
29 *The Works of John Wesley*, Vol. IX, 456.
30 *The Works of John Wesley*, Vol. VII, 199.
31 Colin W. Williams, *John Wesley's Theology Today*, (Nashville: Abingdon Press, MCML), 65.
32 *The Works of John Wesley*, VII, 199.
33 Williams, *John Wesley's Theology Today*, 65.
34 *Wesley's Works*, Vol. 8, 472ff.
35 Williams, *John Wesley's Theology Today*, 66.
36 Lovett H. Weems, *John Wesley's Message Today* (Nashville: Abingdon Press, 1982), 64ff.
37 Watson, *The Message of the Wesleys*, 46.
38 "The Nature of Enthusiasm," *Forty-Four Sermons*, (London: Epworth Press, 1964), 419ff.
39 Ibid., 472, 473.
40 *The Works of John Wesley*, Vol. VIII, 270.
41 Ibid., 250.
42 Lovett H. Weems, *John Wesley's Message Today*, 47.
43 *The Works of John Wesley*, Vol. VIII, 253f.
44 *The Works of John Wesley*, Vol. VIII, 263.
45 Ibid.
46 Ibid., 255.
47 Albert Cook Outler, *Evangelism in the Wesleyan Spirit*, (Canton, MI: Tidings, 1971) 27.
48 Green, *John Wesley*, (London: CH Kelly, 1891) 78f.
49 Williams, *John Wesley's Theology Today*, 168.

Chapter 2

1 World Population Datasheet 2013, September 2013, http://www.prb.org/Publications/Datasheets/2013/2013-world-population-data-sheet/data-sheet.aspx.
2 Author unknown.
3 J. Oswald Sanders, *Spiritual Leadership*, (Chicago: Moody Publishers, 2007), 17.
4 John Maxwell, *The Maxwell Leadership Bible*, (Nashville: Thomas Nelson Publishers, 2007), 553.
5 Chika Onyeani, "G8 Nations Fail Africa Again," *The African Sun Times*, June 17, 2004, as quoted in *Against All Hope: Hope for Africa*, by Darrow L. Miller with Scott Allen and the African Working Group of Samaritan Strategy Africa (Phoenix: Disciple Nations Alliance, 2005), 11.
6
7 Darrow L Miller and Scott Allen, *Against All Hope*, 35.
8 Ibid.
9 Abram Kidd, "Africa's Future Church: Part II," Africa Inland Mission, www.aimint.org/can/en/see/stories/123-africas-future-church-part-ii.

Chapter 3

1 David Watson, *I Believe in Evangelism*, (Grand Rapids: William B. Eerdmans, 1976), 38.
2 Stephen Jay, *La Doctrine Méthodiste*, Eglise Protestante Méthodiste de Côte d'Ivoire, 1990, 9.
3 Ibid., 9.
4 Ibid., 15.
5 Ibid.,18.
6 Ibid., 21.
7 Jon Tal Murphree, *Responsible Evangelism: Relating Theory to Practice*, (Toccoa Falls, Georgia: Toccoa Falls College Press 1998), 13.
8 White River Methodist Church, www.wrmc.co.za/commissions.html.
9 "Coast region medical camp," Methodist Church in Kenya, October 21, 2012, www.methodistchurchkenya.org/index.php/component/content/article/49-activities/84-coast-region-medical-camp.html.
10 Ibid.
11 The Very Reverend Marcel Sachou, conversation with author, at the Sixth Conference of EMU-CI, Côte d'Ivoire, August 2010.
12 "Evangelism," Cry Cameroon Ministries (USA), www.crycameroon.org/pages/evangelism.htm.
13 Roger Yao, et al., "Canevas de formation aux techniques de l'évangélisation," (unpublished manuscript, 2009), Cellulle d'Evangelisation Classique.
14 "World Urbanization Prospects: the 2007 Revision," United Nations Population Division, www.un.org/esa/population/publications/wup2007/2007wup.htm.
15 Ibid.

Chapter 4

1 *The Book of Discipline of the United Methodist Church*, (Nashville: United Methodist Publishing House, 2013).
2 "National Youth Policy: A Vision for the 21st Century," Republic of Uganda, Ministry of Gender, Labour and Social Development, 2001, http://planipolis.iiep.unesco.org/upload/Youth/Uganda/Uganda National Youth Policy.pdf.
3 "Youth," UNESCO Social and Human Services, http://www.unesco.org/new/en/social-and-human-sciences/themes/youth/youth-definition.
4 John Wesley Kurewa, *Drumbeats of Salvation in Africa*, (Mutare: Mutare Garments Ltd., 2007), 14.
5 George G. Hunter, *The Apostolic Congregation, Church Growth Reconceived for a New Generation*, (Nashville: Abingdon Press, 2009), 4.
6 "What is patriarchy?" London Feminist Network, http://londonfeministnetwork.org.uk/home/patriarchy.
7 Debra Simpson, MCC *Gender and Development Project*, (Mennonite Central Committee, 1998) 12.
8 National Youth Policy, Republic of Uganda.
9 Ibid.

10 Ibid.
11 Jeff Andrew Lule, "62% of Ugandan youth jobless—report," *New Vision*, February 1, 2013, http://www.newvision.co.ug/news/639446-62-of-ugandan-youth-jobless--report.html.
12 Jacob Omolo, "Youth Employment in Kenya: Analysis of Labour Market and Policy Interventions," October 2012, http://www.fes-kenya.org/media/publications/2012/FES Occasional paper no.1.
13 "Rwanda: A deprived youth, despite the country's economic growth," *Jambonews*, April 13, 2013, http://www.jambonews.net/en/news/20130413-rwanda-a-deprived-youth-despite-the-countrys-economic-growth.

Chapter 5

1 "Plenary" means the whole Scripture is inspired (1 Timothy 3:16).
2 "Verbal" means the very words of the Bible are inspired (2 Peter 1:20, 21).
3 "Inspired" means, God breathed (1 Timothy 3:16).
4 "Infallible" implies that the information, historical, geographical, scientific, and spiritual in the Bible is true.
5 Homer Duncan, *Wonderful Words of Life*, (Lubbock, Texas: MC International Publications, 1988), 38.
6 Ibid., 45.
7 Gerald T. Sheppard, "The Bible," *Eerdmans Dictionary of the Bible*, edited by David Noel Freedman, Allen C. Myers and Astrid B. Beck, (Grand Rapids: William B. Eerdmans Publishing Company, 2002), 178.
8 Bruce M. Metzger, "To The Reader," *The New Interpreters Study Bible: New Revised Standard Version With the Apocrypha*, (Nashville: Abingdon Press, 2003).
9 Homer Duncan, *Wonderful Words of Life*, 53.
10 Ibid., 55.
11 David J. Bosch, *Transforming Mission: Paradigm Shifts in Theology of Mission*, (New York: Orbis Books, 1991), 58.
12 Ibid., 59.
13 Ibid.
14 Eric Meyers, "Galilee" *Harpers Collins Bible Dictionary*, (New York: HarperOne, 2011), 359.
15 Robert H. Mounce, *New International Biblical Commentary: Matthew (New International Biblical Commentary)*, (London: Hendrickson Publishers, 1991), 268.

Chapter 6

1 John W. Wimberly, Jr., *The Business of the Church: The Uncomfortable Truth that Faithful Ministry Requires Effective Management*, (Herndon, Va.: The Alban Institute, 2010), 8.
2 Ibid., 9-19.
3 Ibid., 19-30.
4 Ibid., 32.

5 Ibid., 33.
6 Ibid., 35.
7 Ibid., 35.
8 Ibid., 3.
9 Ibid., 2.
10 Ibid., 39.
11 Ibid., 42.
12 Ibid., 45.
13 Ibid., 46.
14 Ibid., 49.
15 Ibid., 53.
16 Lovett H. Weems, Jr., "Effective and Visionary Leadership: D.Min. Lectures on Church Leadership Excellency," (lecture, Wesley Theological Seminary, Washington, D.C., May 2010).
17 Lovett H. Weems, Jr., *Church Leadership: Vision, Team, Culture and Integrity*, (Nashville: Abingdon Press, 1993).
18 Lovett Weems, "Effective and Visionary Leadership."
19 "Africa," CIA World Factbook, accessed on January 23, 2014, www.cia.gov/library/publications/the-world-factbook/geos/eg.html.
20 John C. Maxwell, *The 21 Irrefutable Laws of Leadership* (Nashville: Thomas Nelson, 1998), 20
21 Norman J. Cohen, *Moses and the Journey to Leadership*, (Woodstock: Jewish Light Publishing, 2008), 91.
22 Lovett H. Weems Church Leadership: *Vision, Team, Culture and Integrity*, 99.
23 Lovett H. Weems, "Effective and Visionary Leadership."
24 Blaine McCormick and David Davenport, *Shepherd Leadership* (San Francisco: Jossey-Bass, 2003), 7.
25 Lewis A. Parks and Bruce C. Birch, *Ducking Spears, Dancing Madly*, (Nashville: Abingdon Press, 2004), 85.
26 John C. Maxwell, *The 21 Irrefutable Laws of Leadership*, 31.
27 Norman J. Cohen, *Moses and the Journey to Leadership*, 31-32.

Chapter 7

1 "Democratic Republic of Congo," CIA World Factbook, https://www.cia.gov/library/publications/the-world-factbook/geos/cg.html.
2 Congolese National Ministry of Planning, 2005 Report.
3 "Democratic Republic of Congo," CIA World Factbook, https://www.cia.gov/library/publications/the-world-factbook/geos/cg.html.
4 Mande Muyombo, *The Role of the Church in Resolving the Mai-Mai Conflict in North Katanga in the* DR *Congo*, (Africa University, 2006).
5 Ibid.
6 Ibid.

7 R. Scott Appleby, *The Ambivalence of the Sacred: Religion, Violence and Reconciliation*, (Lanham, MD: Rowman & Littlefield Publishers, 2000), 8.
8 Ibid., 28,29.
9 Etienne Tshisekedi was the main opposition leader and president of the Democratic Union for Social Progress; he was seen as the main challenger of Joseph Kabila in the November 2011 Presidential Elections.
10 Michael Perry Kweku Okyerefo et al., *Religion as a Tool in Strengthening the Democratic Process in Ghana*, (University of Ghana, June 2011), 125.
11 Ibid.
12 R. Scott Appleby, *The Ambivalence of the Sacred*, 29
13 Ibid., 30.
14 David C. Rapoport and Leonard Weimberg, *The Democratic Experience and Political Violence*, (London: Frank Cass, 2001).
15 Ibid., 23.
16 Ibid., 51.
17 Ibid.
18 David C. Rapoport and Leonard Weimberg, *The Democratic Experience*,18
19 Ibid.,16.
20 Ibid., 20.
21 Matthias Basedau and Alexander De Juan, *The 'Ambivalence of the Sacred' in Africa: The Impact of Religion on Peace and Conflict in Sub-Saharan Africa*, German Institute of Global and Area Studies. GIGA Research Programme: Violence, Power and Security, March 2008, 6
22 Ibid.
23 R. Scott Appleby, *The Ambivalence of the Sacred*.
24 Matthias Basedau and Alexander De Juan, *The Ambivalence of the Sacred in Africa*, 7.
25 Ibid.
26 Ibid.
27 Ibid.
28 Most *Lubas* of Katanga see themselves as the Jews of DR Congo whom God has chosen to lead. In this regard Bishop Ntambo will always say that in heaven there is only one language which is Kiluba.
29 Ibid., 7.
30 Ibid.
31 Ibid.
32 R. Scott Appleby, *The Ambivalence of the Sacred*, 212.
33 Ibid.
34 Ibid.
35 Ibid., 217.
36 Ibid., 218.
37 Ibid., 233.
38 Ibid., 236.

CPSIA information can be obtained
at www.ICGtesting.com
Printed in the USA
LVOW04s0734280816
502106LV00001B/3/P

9 780881 777451